Edward Maitland

Jewish Literature and Modern Education

Or, the Use and Misuse of the Bible in the Schoolroom

Edward Maitland

Jewish Literature and Modern Education
Or, the Use and Misuse of the Bible in the Schoolroom

ISBN/EAN: 9783337099671

Printed in Europe, USA, Canada, Australia, Japan

Cover: Foto ©Lupo / pixelio.de

More available books at **www.hansebooks.com**

AND

MODERN EDUCATION:

OR,

THE USE AND MISUSE OF THE BIBLE IN THE SCHOOLROOM.

BY THE AUTHOR OF "THE PILGRIM AND THE SHRINE," ETC

(PREVIOUSLY PRINTED FOR PRIVATE CIRCULATION)

"These were more noble than those in Thessalonica, in that they . . . searched the Scriptures daily, whether those things were so."—Acts xvii. 11.

PREFACE.

WHETHER or not the Solution, given in these Lectures, of the "Religious Difficulty" in our National Education, be acceptable for practical application, is a question other than that of the intrinsic soundness of that Solution. It is to this only that my responsibility extends. The responsibility of declining to accept a proffered remedy must rest with those to whom the offer is made.

I had intended to keep these Lectures in manuscript, and repeat them wherever an audience might be found desirous of hearing facts stated without respect to aught but the facts. It is in compliance with very many and pressing solicitations that I have, by printing them, withdrawn them from further delivery as Public Lectures. My hope now is that the readers will not be less numerous than the hearers would have been, had I adhered to my original intention.

The Lectures are printed with the changes made on their second delivery, in Edinburgh. I cannot let them go from me without acknowledging my obligations to the series of small publications issued periodically by Mr Thomas Scott of Ramsgate, to whose indefatigable self devotion to the cause of "Free Inquiry and Free Expression," the present rapid spread of information, and consequent movement of thought on religious matters, especially among the clergy of the Establishment,—(a movement far greater than the public is aware of)—is in no small degree attributable. The tracts entitled, *The Defective Morality of the New Testament*, by Professor F. W. Newman; *The Gospel of the Kingdom*, and *The Influence of Sacred History on the Intellect and Conscience*,—especially deserve mention for the use I have made of them. A few brief passages given as quotations, but without reference, are for the most part taken, with more or less exactness, from *The Pilgrim and the Shrine*. E. M.

LONDON, *September* 1871.

SYNOPSIS.

LECTURE THE FIRST.

SECTION		PAGE
1.	INTRODUCTION,	1
2.	DEFINITION AND FUNCTION OF EDUCATION,	3
3.	THE SCHOOL BOARDS AND THE "RELIGIOUS DIFFICULTY,"	6
4.	THE GENESIS AND HABITAT OF THE "DIFFICULTY,"	11
5.	THE BIBLE AS A MORAL TEACHER,	12
6.	THE BIBLE AS AN INTELLECTUAL TEACHER,	24
7.	THE BIBLE "WITHOUT NOTE OR COMMENT,"	27
8.	THE GOSPELS AND THE CHARACTER OF JESUS,	35
9.	THE "KINGDOM OF HEAVEN,"	37

LECTURE THE SECOND.

10.	THE NEW TESTAMENT AS A RULE OF LIFE AND FAITH,	41
11.	THE "CONTINUITY OF SCRIPTURE," DOCTRINAL AND OTHER,	48
12.	WHY THE BIBLE SHOULD BE TAUGHT IN OUR SCHOOLS,	57
13.	HOW IT SHOULD BE DEALT WITH,	65
14.	"NOTES AND COMMENTS;" THE PRINCIPLE OF THEIR CONSTRUCTION,	69
15.	BIBLICAL INFALLIBILITY,	74
16.	BIBLICAL INSPIRATION,	78
17.	THE BIBLE AND MODERN COMMENTATORS,	86
18.	THE BIBLE AND MODERN PRACTICE,	88
19.	THE SCHOOL AND TEACHER OF THE FUTURE,	94

CORRECTIONS.

Page 14, line 1, *for* xxxvii. *read* xxxviii.
 „ line 3, *for* ix. *read* xi.
Page 31, line 5 from bottom, *for* Gen. *read* Jer.
Page 36, *add as footnote,* See also Luke ix. 60-62, and Mark ii. 27, for harsh utterances ascribed to Jesus.
Page 61, line 14, *put* " *after* intelligence.
Page 63, line 13, *put* are *before* book.
Page 92, *add as footnote,* See also Luke xxiv. 39. Acts xii 15
Page 97, line 3, *omit* " *after* all.

LECTURE THE FIRST.

I.

WHY is it with us in England, that with all our achievements in Science, Literature, and Art; in Government, Industry, and Warfare; in Honour, Religion, and Virtue; with conquests ranging over the whole threefold domain of Humanity, the Physical, the Intellectual, and the Moral,—why is it that the moment we attempt to extend the manifold blessings of our civilisation to the entire mass of our countrymen, we find ourselves at fault and utterly baffled?

Long has the condition of myriads among us been known to be terrible in its degradation. Long have we acknowledged an earnest desire to raise them out of that condition. Measure after measure have we devised and enacted; but none of them, not even the vast Church-establishment of the realm, has proved in any degree commensurate with the evil. At length our efforts have culminated in the elaboration and enactment of one comprehensive scheme; and we have proceeded so far as to have elected as our representatives to carry it into effect, those of us whom, for superior intelligence and energy, we deem best qualified for the task.

Shortlived, however, do our exultant hopes promise to

be. The very agents of our beneficent intentions, the Schoolboards, in whose hands are borne the germs of our redemption and future civilisation, are altogether at such odds within themselves upon some of the leading and most essential principles, that the scheme threatens wholly to collapse in disheartening failure, or to become a perennial source of bitterness and dissension.

Is it not passing strange? Based though our culture has for centuries been, upon one and the self-same book, so far from our having attained any degree of unity thereby, we are divided and rent into sects and factions innumerable and irreconcilable, until it would appear as if the very spirit of that proverbially perverse and stiff-necked people whose sacred literature we have adopted as the rule of our faith and practice, had passed into ourselves and become a constituent part of our very nature.

The greatness of the emergency,—for it is the redemption of our masses from pauperism, ignorance, and barbarism that is at stake,—not justifies merely, but imperatively demands the strenuous collaboration of all who, having the good of their kind at heart, have made this question one of special investigation. It is in no spirit of hasty presumption,— scarcely is it with much hope of wide acceptance,—at least in the present,—that I have responded to the invitation to recite here to-day the conclusions to which my study of the points at issue has brought me. Rather is it that it will be a relief to myself to have thrown off the reflections and results which, in a somewhat varied experience at home and abroad, have accumulated upon me, and to feel that I have done this at the time when there is most chance of their being useful. It is thus that I have prepared my contribution towards the solution of "the Religious Difficulty" which lies "a lion in the path" of our National Education and all our national improvement, showing as yet not the smallest symptom of discomposure through any "Resolution" of Metropolitan or other School-board.

II.

In all emergencies, whether of conduct or of opinion, where there is doubt and space for deliberation, it is best to go back to the very beginning of the matter, and there, in its initial principles, seek the clue which is to conduct us safely out of our dilemma. It is wonderful sometimes how readily a skein is disentangled when once the right end of the thread has been found. Our friends across the Atlantic, the Americans, were for a long time disastrously hampered in their attempts at legislation. It is not surprising that it should have been so, when we consider that the principal object of legislation is Man, and that the two great sections of the American community differed altogether in their definition of Man; the one holding that persons who had dark complexions and a peculiar kind of rough curly hair, several millions of whom lived in the country, were not men; and the other holding that they were just as much entitled to be treated as human beings as people with light complexions and smooth hair. At length, after many years of bitter quarrelling, ending with one of the most fearful internecine conflicts ever known, it was agreed to regard all people as human, and to legislate alike for them with perfect equality; whereupon the difficulty entirely vanished, and the course of the nation became smooth and easy.

In like manner our difficulties, in regard to popular

instruction, have all arisen through our neglect of a definition. We have not defined to ourselves the precise object of the system of National Education, which, after generations of anxious endeavour, we have at length succeeded in obtaining, and which we are now seeking to bring into operation throughout the length and breadth of the land.

The first step towards obtaining what we want, ever is to know what we want; and since in this case we cannot purchase the article ready-made, but have to fabricate it for ourselves, it is not sufficient to have a bare name for it, or a vague apprehension about it, but we must be conversant with its nature, characteristics, and uses.

Let us further simplify and enlarge the scope of the question, and ask what is the object of all the education, public or private, which we give, or seek to give, to our children? What, in short, is the purpose of education?

Using the term education in its broad sense, and without reference to technical instruction in special subjects, we can only answer, that its purpose is to make children into good and capable men and women by cultivating their intelligence and their moral sense, or conscience.

It follows, if we agree to this definition, that we are bound to reject as worse than useless, any instruction which is calculated to repress or pervert either of those faculties from their proper healthy development.

Those who at first hesitate to acquiesce in this definition, in the belief that education should have a more special object, such as to make good Christians, good Catholics, good Protestants, good Churchmen, or good Nonconformists, must on a little reflection perceive that they cannot really mean to rank the intelligence and moral sense as secondary and subordinate to such ends, but that they only desire people to be good Christians, good Churchmen, and so on, because the fact of being so would, in their view, involve the best culture of the faculties in question. So that if they believed it did not involve this end, they would abandon their preference for such denominations. That is, they would rather have people to be good men and bad (say) Nonconformists, than good Nonconformists and bad men.

Agreeing, then, that the object of education is the development of the intellect and moral sense, we shall, no doubt, further agree that the best chance of successfully cultivating those desirable qualities which we designate *virtues*, lies in impressing the mind while young with the most elevated and winning examples of them, and guarding it from any familiarity with their opposites; and that it is because we deem such qualities to be best, that we regard the Deity as possessing them in the Infinite, and hold up as a pattern of life the most perfect example of them in the finite.

Yet, though agreeing both in the object and method of education when thus plainly put before us, so ingeniously perverse and inconsistent are we that we first refuse to agree upon any common system of instruction whatever, and then we insist upon neutralising or vitiating such instruction as we do agree upon, by mingling it with teaching which is at once repressive of the Intellect, and injurious to the Moral Sense.

The sole impediment to the success of our efforts, the rock upon which all our hopes of rescuing the mass of our countrymen from ignorance and barbarism are in danger of being dashed, consists in the unreasoning and indiscriminate veneration in which the Bible is popularly held among us. Impelled by that veneration, we hesitate not to degrade our children's view of Deity by familiarising them with a literature in which He is represented as feeble, treacherous, implacable, and unjust; and confound at once their Intelligence and Moral Sense, by compelling them to regard that literature as altogether divine and infallible.

Strange infatuation and inconsistency, if, after toiling for years to obtain an effective system of national education, we either abandon the task as hopeless, or insist upon accompanying it by teaching which involves a fatal outrage upon the very intellect and conscience which it is the express purpose of that education to foster and develop!

III.

Before considering the action of the School-boards, I must advert for a moment to the principle of their constitution.

There is this difference between Government by Representation and Government by Delegation. It is the duty of the mere delegate to vote on any given question precisely as a majority of his constituents may instruct him. The deliberative function rests with them. He is their faithful, but unintelligent instrument. The representative, on the contrary, is selected on account of his superior faculties or attainments, to go on behalf of his constituents to the headquarters of information, and there, in conference with other selected intellects, form the best judgment in his power; his constituents determining only the general principles and direction of his policy.

The School-boards which are charged with the determination of our new educational system, having been selected on this principle of representation, we are entitled to look to their superior intelligence to supplement popular deficiencies; to be superior to popular prejudices; to be teachers, and, if need be, rebukers, rather than followers and flatterers of the less instructed masses: and it is due to such bodies that we carefully examine the methods by which they propose to deal with existing difficulties.

Those difficulties turning exclusively upon Religion, one great step towards their solution has been gained by the agreement to exclude from the common schools such minor subjects of difference as the creeds and catechisms of particular denominations. The Bible remains, the sole stumbling-block and rock of offence.

The London Board may be taken as representative not only of the largest and most intelligent body of constituents, but also of all the other School-boards. I propose, therefore, to deal with the propositions by which the members of that Board have sought to meet the "religious difficulty." They are six in number:

1. That the Bible be excluded altogether, on the ground that its admission is inconsistent with religious equality.

2. That the Bible be admitted and read, but without note or comment.

3. That the Bible be read for the purpose of religious culture, at the discretion of the teacher.

4. That the teacher's discretion in the use of the Bible be so restricted as to exclude the distinctive doctrines of any sect.

5. That no principle respecting the use of the Bible

be laid down, but that each separate school be dealt with by itself.

6. That the Bible be read with such explanations in matters of language, history, customs, &c., as may be needed to make its meaning plain; and that there be given such instruction in its teaching, on the first principles of morality and religion, as is suitable to the capacities of children; always excluding denominational teaching.

The Fifth Resolution, "that no principle be laid down," aptly describes the condition of the question up to that point. In the absence of a definition of its object, it was impossible for the Board to lay down any principle for its guidance. In the absence of any controlling definition, it could only look back to its constituents to see what they would bear from it. And looking to the confused mass of public opinion and prejudice in the absence of any light of one's own, is like shutting one's eyes to avoid seeing the dark.

Travelling one day by a railway on which there are several tunnels, I observed that whenever the train entered a tunnel, a little boy who sat next to me, immediately pressed his hands over his eyes, and buried his face in the cushions. To my inquiry why he did this, he answered that it was because he was afraid of the dark. I asked him whether it was not just as dark to him when his face was buried in the cushions. He said yes; but he had not thought of that, and he would not know now what to do. I could not bear to deprive him of his faith, however unenlightened, without giving him another. A lamp was burning in the roof of the carriage, too dim in the broad daylight to have attracted his attention, yet bright enough to dispel the gloom of the tunnel. I suggested that, instead of covering his face, he would do better to keep his eyes fixed on the lamp. The little fellow brightened with joy at the thought; and during the rest of the journey, the instant we entered a tunnel, there he was, no longer fearful and burying himself in deeper darkness, but steadfastly looking to the light that shone above him.

"Look to the light!" is no bad maxim even for those who have to determine grave questions for the benefit of others. We have but to "look to the light" of the definition we have already agreed upon, and difficulties fly like darkness before the approaching dawn. Even the difficulties themselves, like Daphne before the Sungod, are apt to turn into flowers for our delectation.

The Sixth Resolution, that proposed by Dr Angus, and supported by Professor Huxley, is the first that shows any consciousness that there is a light to which we may look for encouragement and guidance. "That instruction should be given in the Bible *on the first principles of morality and religion.*" According to our definition, Education consists in the cultivation of the Intelligence and the Moral Sense. This is the light on which the gaze must be so steadily fixed, that no conflicting influences shall be capable of diverting our attention. Interpreted by it, the Bible itself bears witness to the way in which it should be used. Here, in full accordance with it, is one of its utterances, "God is no respecter of persons; but in every nation, he that feareth Him and worketh righteousness, is accepted with Him." (Acts x. 34-5.) Acting in this spirit, our School-boards will be no respecters of authors or books, but in every writing that, and that only, "which feareth God and worketh righteousness," shall be accepted by them. Here is another, also on the positive side: "Whatsoever things are true, whatsoever things are honest, whatsoever things are just, whatsoever things are pure, whatsoever things are lovely, whatsoever things are of good report; if there be any virtue, and if there be any praise, think on these things." (Phil. iv. 8.) And another seems to define that Scripture or writing, as alone given by a holy inspiration, which "is profitable for doctrine, for reproof, for correction, for instruction in righteousness." (2 Tim. iii. 16.) And on the negative side we have "Refuse profane and old wives' fables;" (1 Tim. iv. 7.) "not giving heed to Jewish fables." (Titus i. 14.) "But all uncleanness let it not be once named among you;" "for it is a shame even to speak of those things which are done of them in secret." (Eph. v. 3, 12.) And one more on the positive side. "Whatsoever ye do, do all to the *glory* of God." (1 Cor. x. 31.)

Yet with these plain rules for our guidance, not one of the resolutions proposes to place any restriction upon the use of the Bible by the children. One, indeed, proposes to exclude it bodily from the schools, the good and the evil together, but upon grounds in no way connected with its fitness for the perusal of youth. And even the resolution finally accepted by the Board, while ambiguously proposing "to give from the Bible such instruction in the principles of religion and morality as is suitable to the capacities of children," ventures on no protest against the Bible as it now stands being put into the hands of children at all.

The fact is, that the members have allowed themselves to be so exclusively guided by the "winds" of popular "doctrine," that they "have omitted the weightier matters of the law" of morality, and "passed over judgment and the love of God."

IV.

The reason is not far to seek. A representative body would not be representative were any wide interval to intervene between its own intelligence and attainments and those of its constituents. The latter can be guided in their selection only by the light they possess; not by that which they do not possess. Wherefore, for the School-board to have passed any more radical Resolution than that which it did pass, would have been for it to have made itself, not the representative, but the independent superior of the body which elected it. The primary defect, therefore, lies with the people at large. It is the vast amount of bigoted ignorance and superstition still remaining among us that constitutes the real obstacle to any sound system of national education. It is the elders who require to be instructed, before we can begin to teach the children. It is true that a transition has begun. But every step of the progress from the old to the new, from darkness to light, is so vehemently opposed by the vested interests of the dead past, that the patience of those who believe in the possibility of progress may well be exhausted, and their faith quenched in despair.

To be effectual, therefore, remonstrance must be addressed to the people at large, rather than to their representatives on the School-boards. The transition of which I spoke as having already begun, is the transition from a morality affecting to be based upon theology, to a religion really based upon morality, and, consequently, to a sound system of morality. This transition must attain a far more advanced stage in its progress before the School-board can even begin to carry out the Re-

solution it has passed. It is absolutely impossible to
"give from the Bible, instruction in the principles of
morality and religion suitable to children," until the
popular theory respecting the Bible, and the theology
based upon it, is so vastly modified as to amount to
an almost total renunciation of that theory. The absolute and irreconcilable antagonism between what is
called Biblical Theology and the modern principles of
"Religion and Morality," cannot be too distinctly
asserted or loudly proclaimed, if we sincerely desire
our children to have an education really consisting in
the development of their intelligence and moral sense.

Valuing the Bible highly as I do, for very much
that is very valuable in it, it is no grateful task to have
to search out and expose the characteristics which
render it an unsuitable basis for the instruction of
children, whether in morality or in religion. Such ex-
posure, however, being indispensable to the solution of
the problem of our national education, to shrink from
it would be to abandon that problem as insoluble, that
education as impossible.

V.

Bearing always in mind our definition of the purpose
and method of education, namely the development of
the intelligence and moral sense by the inculcation of
"the true, the pure, and the honest,"—bearing in mind
also the fundamental fact in human nature, that man's
view of Deity inevitably reacts upon himself, tending
to form him in the image of his own ideal,—it is self-
evident that to familiarise children with the imperfect
morality, the coarse manners and expressions, the rude

fables, and the degrading ideas of Deity, appertaining to a people low in culture—such as were the Israelites—and to confound their minds and consciences at the most impressible period of life by telling them that such narratives and representations are all divinely inspired and infallibly true,—is to utterly stultify ourselves and the whole of the principles by which we profess to be actuated in giving them an education at all. Did we find any others than ourselves, say South Sea savages, putting into the hands of their children, books containing coarse and impure stories, detailing the morbid anatomy of the most execrable vices, extolling deeds prompted by a spirit of the lowest selfishness, exulting in fraud, rapine, and murder, and justifying whatever is most disgraceful to humanity by representing it as prompted or approved by their Deity, and so making Him altogether such an one as themselves,—surely we should say that they must indeed be savages of the lowest and most degraded type, and sad proofs of the utter depravity of human nature.

In investigating from our present point of view the contents of this most read, yet most misread, of books, we must dismiss from our minds any idea that its most objectionable features are amenable to revision or re-translation. The faults thus removable are but as freckles upon the skin compared with a constitutional taint. For it is the spirit as well as the letter of a large portion of it, that whether "for reproof, for correction, or for instruction in righteousness," is hopelessly in fault: and the spirit of a book is of infinitely greater importance than its superficial details.

Palpable to the eyes of all are the hideous tales of Lot and his daughters; (Gen. xix.) Judah and Tamar;

(xxxvii.) the massacre of the Shechemites; (xxxiv.) the Levite of Ephraim; (Jud. xix.) David and Bathsheba; (2 Sam. ix.) Amnon and his sister; (xiii.) and whole chapters in Leviticus and the Prophets. That such things should be in a book given freely to children to read, and that they should be expected notwithstanding to grow up pure and uncontaminated in mind and habit, is one of those anomalies in the British character which makes it a hopeless puzzle to the world. Who can say that much of the viciousness at present prevalent among us, is not attributable to early curiosity being aroused and stimulated by the obscenities of the Old Testament? To put the Bible as it is into the hands of our children, is not only totally to bewilder their sense of right and wrong,—it is to invite familiarity with the idea of the worst Oriental vices.

Even in the case of those vices being mentioned only to be denounced, the suggestion is apt to remain, and the denunciation to be disregarded. It notoriously is injudicious to put into the minds of children faults of which they might never have thought themselves, for the sake of admonishing them against them. It is related somewhere that a catalogue of offences punishable by law was once posted in the Roman forum as a warning to the citizens; but that this was followed by such a vast increase in the number and variety of the crimes committed, that it was found advisable to remove it. I myself know an instance of a pious mother sending her daughter to a boarding-school, having first written in her Bible a list of the chapters and passages which she was not to read. It is remarkable how popular in the school that particular Bible became. The other girls were always borrowing it. There is no reason to suppose that boys would have acted differently.

It is true that the particular instances I have adduced may not be immoral as they stand in the Bible, but they are assuredly provocative of immorality in children who read them. A far more serious indictment against the Bible as a handbook of moral instruction must be founded on its habit of representing the Deity as a consenting party to some of the worst actions of its characters: nay, so unreliable is it as a basis of anything whatever, that after thus characterising the Deity, it deals in strong denunciations against those "who not only commit such things themselves, but have pleasure in them that do them;" (Rom. i. 32.) thus, by direct implication condemning the Deity Himself. If it be desirable to impress upon children the belief that only those "who fear God and work righteousness are acceptable to him," it is to stultify the whole principle of their education to represent Him to them as an eastern monarch, selecting his favourites by caprice, and independently of any merit or demerit on their part. Yet the entire Bible rests upon the idea that so far from being an equal Father of all, "whose tender mercies are over all His works," (Ps. cxlv. 9.) the Almighty selected out of all mankind one race to be "His own peculiar people," (Deut. xiv. 9.) and out of that race certain individuals to be His own peculiar favourites, and this in spite of the most glaring defects in their characters and conduct; and sustained those whom He had thus chosen through the whole course of their misdeeds.

Thus, Abraham is said to have had "faith," and this faith is said to have been "imputed to him for righteousness;" (Rom. iv. 22.) but how far was his actual conduct righteous, and how much faith did it imply? Assured by repeated promises of the divine favour and protection, as well as of a great posterity through his then childless wife Sarai, he twice voluntarily prostituted her to Pagan chieftains, pretending that she was *only* his sister. And we read that "the Lord plagued,"—not the liar and poltroon who thus degraded his wife, and entrapped the kings, whose hospitality he was enjoying;—not the wife so extraordinarily ready to "obey her husband in all things;" (it appears that her age was about sixty-five on one occasion, and ninety on the other);—but "the Lord plagued Pharaoh and Abimelech with great plagues because of Sarai, Abraham's wife," and in the case of the latter, would only grant forgiveness upon the intercession of Abraham, saying, "for he is a prophet." (Gen. xii. 20.) Isaac, we read, copied the twice committed fault of his father, in passing off his wife Rebekah as his sister upon another king, and was divinely blessed notwithstanding. In short, in all three transactions, out of the whole of the parties to them, Abraham, Isaac, Sarai, Rebekah, the three kings, and the Deity, those only who indicate the possession of any moral sense whatever are the Pagan kings, who show it in no small degree, and these alone are punished; while Abraham and Isaac retain the divine favour throughout, the former being honoured by the distinctive title of "Friend of God." (James ii. 23.)

The selfishness and cowardice of Abraham are still farther illustrated by his treatment of Hagar and Ishmael. There is no reason to doubt the perfect truthfulness of the Bible narrative in respect to *him*. But when it goes on to represent the Deity as encouraging him in his cruel and unfatherly conduct to his son, and bidding him follow the lead of a frivolous and heartless wife;—"In all that Sarai hath said unto thee, hearken unto her voice;" (Gen. xxi. 12.) then our moral sense is offended, and we refuse to identify the God of Abraham with the God of our own clearer perceptions.

The utter indifference of " the God of Abraham, Isaac, and Jacob" to any moral law whatever, reaches its climax in the history of Jacob. A liar and a trickster from early youth, yet constantly enjoying the presence and approbation of God, who finds no word or sign of reproach wherewith to touch his conscience or arouse his fears,—such is the patriarch whom the Bible sets forth as one of God's especial favourites, because, forsooth, he had " faith." In presence of this mystic quality, right and wrong sink into absolute nothingness; and that most fatal of all impieties, a total divorce between the will of God and the moral law, finds its plea and justification. It is little that I would give for the moral sensibility of the child who could read without a pang of indignation and a tear of pity the tale of this ingrained blackleg's atrocities; his taking advantage of his rough, honest-hearted brother's extremity of exhaustion through hunger to extort from him his birthright; (Gen. xxv.) his heartless deception of his poor, blind old father; (xxvii.) his repeated cheats, thefts, and falsehoods against his father-in-law; (xxx., &c.) and the divine confirmation to him of the blessings thus fraudulently acquired; " yea, and he shall be blessed," and constant assurance of the divine presence and approbation.

It is without a word of repudiation that the Bible acquiesces in Jacob's degradation of the Deity to a huckstering or bargaining God; a God, too, who can be got the better of in a business transaction. For, " Jacob vowed a vow, saying, If God will be with me in this way that I go, and will give me bread to eat and raiment to put on, so that I come again to my father's house in peace; *then* shall the Lord be my God; and this stone which I have set for a pillar shall be God's house; and of *all* that thou shalt give me I will surely give the *tenth* unto thee." (xxviii. 20, &c.)

When the Israelites reach the Promised Land, their "sacred history" consists of little beside perpetual butcheries. The more directly they are represented as being under divine guidance, the more sanguinary is their career. Slaughter of men, women, children, infants at the breast. None spared, none, except, sometimes—and mark the exception made by the followers, not of Mahomet, but of Jehovah—the unmarried girls. Every sentiment of humanity and mercy is accounted an unpardonable weakness. Jehovah appears as a savage patriot-God, approving impurity, treachery, murder, and whatever else was perpetrated on the side of his "chosen people." A Bushman of South Africa being once asked to define the difference between good and evil, replied, "It is good when I steal another man's wives; evil when another man steals mine." Such is precisely the standard of right and wrong laid down by the Bible in respect to the Israelites and their neighbours. Can we wonder that recent moralists have written to vindicate the Almighty from the aspersions cast upon his character in the Bible.[*]

In all the events of the late dreadful war upon the Continent, probably no single incident caused such a thrill of horror as that of the wounded German soldier who staggered from the field of battle into a peasant's cottage, and fell fainting upon the bed, and only lived long enough to tell his comrades how that the woman of the cottage had taken advantage of his helpless condition to pick out his eyes with a fork. Possibly the French

[*] *E.g.* Theodore Parker in America, and Dr Perfitt in England.

woman had heard of the blessing pronounced upon Jael for a similar act. Possibly she had learned from "Sacred History" that the most revolting perfidy and cruelty become heroic virtues when exercised upon one's own side. And were not we Europeans of to-day, with all our faults, infinitely in advance of those bad times, we too might find a patriot-poet rivalling the utterances of the "divinely-inspired" Deborah, to laud the French tigress as the Jewish one was lauded, detail with rapturous glee every particular of the fiendish deed, and mock the wretched victim's mother watching and longing in vain for her murdered son's return.

Nay, the conduct of her whom the Bible pronounces as "blessed above women," was even more flagrant in its utter heinousness than that of the French woman. For the husband of Jael had severed himself from the hostile peoples; "there was peace between Jabin, the King of Hazor, and the house of Heber, the Kenite;" and he dwelt, a friendly neutral, in a region apart. The general Sisera, moreover, utterly beaten and discomfited, had fled expressly to Jael's tent for safety, knowing the family to be friendly, and she had invited him in with assurances of protection. "Turn in, my lord, fear not." (Jud. iv.)

While Abraham is described as "the friend of God," to David is awarded the honour of being styled "a man after God's own heart;" (1 Sam. xiii. 14; Acts xiii. 22.) "who turned not away from anything that he commanded him all the days of his life, save only" in one particular instance. (1 Kings xv. 5.) In order to see how little the Bible is fitted for the instruction of children in respect of a moral sense, let us brush aside for a moment the halo with which the name of David is surrounded, and read his history for ourselves. It is through want of doing this, that a popular writer has recently described his life as uniformly "bright and beautiful up to the time of his one great sin."* Yet, his career, soon after the intrepid act which first brought him into notice, was one of rebellion and brigandage. Collecting all that were in debt, distress, and discontent, (1 Sam. xxii. 2.) he organised them into bands of freebooters to levy blackmail upon the farmers. One of these, named Nabal, when applied to on account of David, boldly and naturally answered, "Who is David? and who is this son of Jesse? there be many servants now-a-days that break away every man from his master. Shall I then take my bread, and my water, and my flesh that I have killed for my shearers, and give it unto men whom I know not whence they be?"

However, Abigail, the wife of Nabal, touched by her servant's account of the gallantry of the band, took of her husband's stores and gave liberally to them. Upon this David assured her that, but for her conduct, he would not have left even a dog of Nabal's household alive by next morning. A few days afterwards Nabal died; the Bible, as if to remove any suspicion of foul play, stating that "the Lord smote him;" when David immediately took Abigail to be his own wife. (1 Sam. xxv.)

When the great contest took place between the Philistines and the Israelites, in which the latter were utterly routed, and Saul and Jonathan, David's bosom friend, were slain, David with his forces stood aloof, unheeding the peril of his countrymen. (1 Sam. xxx.) The crown thus devolved upon Ishbosheth the son of Saul, who was supported by eleven out of the twelve tribes. David,

* Miss Yonge, in "Musings on the Christian Year."

however, would not accept their choice, even though the whole strength of Israel was needed at that critical moment to withstand the Philistines. (2 Sam. ii.) Exciting a civil war, he got himself acknowledged as king by the dissentient tribe of Judah. Treachery and murder came freely to his aid, and he at length found the crown of Israel in his hands. But he felt his tenure of it insecure so long as any descendant of Saul remained to dispute it with him. He therefore concerted with the priests, who, since Saul had slighted their authority, had sided with David, a plot to get rid of the seven sons and grandsons of Saul. The country having been for three years distressed by famine, David consulted the Oracles. In Bible phraseology, he "inquired of the Lord." Of what kind of a Lord he inquired, may be judged by the response. "It is for Saul and his bloody house, because he slew the Gibeonites" many years before. Upon this the Gibeonites, duly instructed, besought of David that, as an "atonement," seven males of Saul's family should be "hanged up unto the Lord." And David took the seven and delivered them into the hands of the Gibeonites, five of them being sons of his own former wife Michal, "and they hanged them in the hill before the Lord. . . . And after that, God was intreated for the land." (2 Sam. xxi. 1-14.) Revolt, treason, murder, human sacrifices, all in the name of "the Lord"!

On one occasion, after defeating the Moabites, David, we read, assembled all the people of that nation on a plain, made them lie down, and divided them into three groups with a line. Two of these groups he put to death, and the other he reduced to slavery. (2 Sam. viii. 2.) The conquered Ammonites he treated with even greater ferocity, tearing and hewing some of them in pieces with harrows, axes, and saws, and roasting others in brickkilns. (xii. 31.) His luxury and voluptuousness equalled his cruelty. Having had seven wives while he ruled over Judah alone, he added to the number all those who had belonged to Saul, (8.) and took yet more wives and concubines after he had come from Hebron. (v. 13.) But these, and his vast pomp, were insufficient to satiate him. Having caught sight of Bathsheba, the wife of one of his captains named Uriah, he took her to himself, and sent Uriah to join the army in the field, giving express orders to his commanding officer to place him in the fore front of the fight to insure his being killed.

It appears that there was then in Israel an honest prophet named Nathan, who had the courage to remonstrate with the king, and who did so with such effect, that David was made, for once, to see the enormity of his conduct. We read, however, that the Lord put away David's sin, so that he did not die. But his child did. And no sooner was the innocent thus punished for the guilty, than "David comforted Bathsheba his wife, and she bare a son, and he called his name Solomon; and the Lord loved him. And he sent by the hand of Nathan the prophet," now subsided into the obsequious court chaplain, "and he called his name Jedidiah," or "Beloved of the Lord." (2 Sam. xii.)

Old age and infirmity wrought no amendment in the truculent spirit of David; a spirit so truculent as to make it morally impossible that he could really have been the author of any of those psalms which in after ages it pleased his countrymen to ascribe to him; excepting only, perhaps, the more ferocious of them. He has been called, "the Byron of the Bible," which, after what has just been stated, seems exceedingly unfair to Byron.

Early in David's career of blood, one Shimei had, in generous indignation, cursed him for his murder of the sons of Saul. (2 Sam. xvi.) He had afterwards begged forgiveness and received it. (xix. 16-23.) Yet David's last instructions to Solomon were in this wise—" Behold thou hast with thee Shimei the son of Gera, which cursed me with a grievous curse in the day when I came to Mahanaim : but he came down to meet me at Jordan, and I sware to him by the Lord, saying, I will not put thee to death with the sword. Now, therefore, hold him not guiltless . . . but his hoar head bring thou down to the grave with blood. So David slept with his fathers." (1 Kings ii. 8-10, &c.) And Solomon "commanded Benaiah, the son of Jehoiada, which went out and fell upon Shimei, that he died." (46.) " And Solomon loved the Lord, walking in the statutes of David, his father." And " the Lord appeared to Solomon in a dream by night ; and God said, ask what I shall give thee. And Solomon said, Thou hast shown unto thy servant David, my father, great mercy, according as he walked before thee in truth, and in righteousness, and in uprightness of heart with thee : and thou hast kept for him this great kindness, that thou hast given him a son to sit on his throne. . . . And God said unto him . . . if thou wilt walk in my ways, to keep my statutes and my commandments, as thy father David did walk, then will I lengthen thy days." (1 Kings iii.)

The mystery of these astounding utterances is not far to seek. History in those days was the work of the sacerdotal class. To support and subserve that class was then, as it has been, for the most part, ever since, to be pronounced, " beloved of the Lord," no matter how evil the individual really was, or how derogatory to the divine honour it might be to have such a preference ascribed to it. To have "faith" in the priests counterbalanced and condoned any quantity of wicked "works." Their standard of right and wrong, good and evil, was that of the Bushman. Whatever was for them was good; whatever was against them was evil. It is, then, for us seriously to ask ourselves whether, when we set before our children as a fit object of worship such a being as the Bible represents the God of Abraham, Isaac, and Jacob, of Samuel, David, and Solomon, to have been, we are ministering towards the end we have in view in giving to them an education; or whether, in place of raising them in the scale of being, we are not rather ministering to the total degradation in them of the human soul.

VI.

These are but a few of the instances in which the Bible is antagonistic to one of the main objects of education, the development of the moral sense. We will now examine how far its teaching is adapted to promote the cultivation of the intellect, still confining ourselves to the Old Testament.

What are the "glorious gains" of the modern mind, of which we are justly proud, and what are the ideas respecting the constitution of the universe, the recognition of which we regard as necessary to entitle any one to the appellation of an intelligent and educated person?

Surely they are that the order of nature is invariable, the whole universe being governed by laws so perfectly appointed as to need no rectification, and fixed so inherently in it as to constitute its nature. That, though incapable of interference from without, inasmuch as there can be no without, all things proceeding from within from its divine immanent character,—its parts are endowed with a capacity of advancing by a process of continual evolution to a degree ever higher of complexity and organisation, as within the physical structure rises the mental, with all its capabilities of moral, intellectual, and spiritual, in grandeur surpassing the majesty of the whole external Cosmos. That it is a low and degrading superstition to regard deity as other than One, ever living and operating equally and impartially throughout the whole domain of existence; or as dwelling apart from the world, and only occasionally giving proof of his being by disturbance of the general order. And that,—while it is impossible truly to ascribe to him aught of feeling corresponding to the love, hate, fear, passion, caprice, appetite, or other affection of men,—when for purposes of instruction or devotion we seek to utilise the anthropomorphic tendency of our nature, He is to be represented as the absolute impersonation of all that we recognise as best in Humanity.

To what depths do we fall when, abandoning these hard-won gains of the Intellect's long warfare against ignorance, barbarism, and superstition, instead of placing our children upon the vantage ground we have acquired, and handing to them our lights at the point which we ourselves have attained, that they may carry them on yet further, we abuse their understandings at the most impressible age, by compelling them to regard the Almighty as no equal God and Father of the whole human race, but the exclusive patron of a small Semitic tribe dwelling in Palestine, whom he supported by prodigies and miracles in their aggressions upon their neighbours, revealing to them alone the light of his word, and condemning all others to enforced darkness. By teaching them to believe in magic and witchcraft, in talismans, charms, and vows; in beasts speaking with human voices and sentiments; (Gen. iii. 1-4; Num. xxii. 28-30.) in a deity writing with a finger; (Ex. xxxi. 18.) speaking with a voice; (xix. 19.) enjoying the smell of roast meat; (Gen. viii. 21.) standing face to face; (xxxii. 30.) walking in a garden; (iii. 8.) revealing his hinder parts; (Ex. xxxiii. 23.) coming down to obtain information as to what men were doing, and to devise measures in accordance therewith; (Gen. xi. 5-7; xviii. 20, 21.) impressing men, not through their consciences, but by signs and wonders, miracles and dreams; recognising and confirming advantages gained by fraud, to the irreparable disadvantage of their rightful owner; (Gen. xxvii. 33-37.) in the case of one deliverer of his chosen people, making his strength depend upon the length of his hair; (Jud. xvi. 17.) allowing another, in virtue of a hasty vow, to offer up his daughter in human sacrifice as a burnt-offering; (xi. 30-39; Num. xxx.) and, lastly, teaching them to believe in man created perfect, and yet unable to resist the first and smallest temptation; and, for such a peccadillo as the eating of the fruit of a magical tree, being with his whole unborn progeny so ferociously damned as to be redeemable only by another human sacrifice, even the stupendous sacrifice of God's only Son.

How utterly bewildering to the expanding intelligence of youth to be told that the God whom they are to worship is revealed in the Bible, and to find him such a being as this! Terrible indeed is their responsibility who proclaim as divinely infallible every absurd or monstrous narrative to be found in the fragmentary legends of a barbarous and imaginative people. When we consider how great is the difficulty of detaching the mind from pernicious ideas when imprinted on it in childhood, and fitting it to receive the later revelations of reason and morality, we can but shudder at the sum of misery undergone in the conflict between the Intellect and the Conscience, through the former having commenced its onward march, while the latter still continues bound to the beliefs of childhood. A very Nessus-shirt of burning poison and agony to all generations of Christendom, has been the garb of ancient faith which we have adopted and worn, in spite of its being totally unfitted to us.

VII.

It is a practice with many savage tribes to invest some object with certain magical properties, altogether independent of its real qualities, and to worship this with a blind adoration, the whole process being known by the name of Fetich worship.

Now what else than precisely such Fetich-worship is theirs who would put up a book to be venerated, but refuse to allow it to be made comprehensible by any kind of interpretation? Yet, of all the Resolutions considered by the School-board, that for which the country at large manifested the strongest preference at the elections was the proposition "that the Bible be read in the schools, but without note or comment."

It can only be the absence of any precise notion as to what education consists in that has prompted a suggestion so utterly opposed to any sort of wholesome development. To suggest difficulties—such difficulties—

and forbid their explanation! Better far that the children read the Bible in the original tongues at once, than in the "authorised version." They might not get much good from the process, but they would assuredly get less harm.

But we will test the working of this suggestion by a few out of the numerous instances of apparent contradiction which, "without note or comment," cannot fail to plunge youthful readers in hopeless perplexity.

And first, concerning the Deity, we read that "God saw everything that he had made, and behold it was very good." (Gen. i. 31.) This was said after the creation of man, when the character and liabilities of that creation must have been fully known to God. Yet we are told soon after that "it repented the Lord that he had made man on the earth, and it grieved him at his heart; (iv. 6.) implying that he was surprised and disappointed at the way man had turned out, having expected better things of him: implying, too, that the divine prescience was at fault, the divine work a failure. And in many other passages we read of the Deity as repenting and changing his mind; being weary and resting. Yet elsewhere in the same book it is declared that "God is not a man that he should repent;" (Num. xxxiii. 19.) being one "with whom is no variableness, neither shadow of turning;" (Jam. i. 17.) "who fainteth not, neither is weary." (Is. xl. 28; also 1 Sam. xv, 35; Jonah iii. 10; Ex. xxxiii. 1; &c.)

Even the all-important questions of God's justice and power remain in suspense with such passages as these unreconciled: "A God of truth and without iniquity, just and right is he." (Deut. xxxii. 4.) "Hear now, O house of Israel; are not my ways equal? are not your ways unequal ? Therefore I will judge you. . . . . every one according to his ways, saith the Lord God." "The son shall not bear the iniquity of the father." (Ez. xviii. 20, 25-30.) And, "I . . . am a jealous God, visiting the iniquity of the fathers upon the children." (Ex. xx. 5.) Also, "For the children being not yet born, neither having done any good or evil, that the purpose of God according to election might stand, not of works, but of him that calleth, it was said unto her (by God), the elder shall serve the younger. As it is written, Jacob have I loved (Jacob ?) but Esau have I hated." (Rom. ix. 11-13 ; Gen. ix. 25 ; Matt. xiii. 11-17.) How, moreover, are children to reconcile this with the declaration that "God is no respecter of persons?" And while, notwithstanding that "with God all things are possible," (Matt. xix. 25.) we are told that "the Lord was with Judah, and he drave out the inhabitants of the mountain ; but could not drive out the inhabitants of the valley, because they had chariots of iron." (Jud. i. 19 ; Josh. xvii. 18.) Also that the inhabitants of Meroz were bitterly cursed "because they came not to the help of the Lord against the mighty." (Jud. v. 23.)

Notwithstanding that we read in several places that God was seen face to face, and his voice heard, (Gen. iii. 9, 10 ; xxxii. 30 ; Ex. xxiv. 9-11 ; xxxiii. 11 ; Is. vi. 1.) we are yet assured that " no man hath seen God at any time ;" (John i. 18.) hath " neither heard his voice at any time, nor seen his face." (v. 37.) And God himself said unto Moses, "Thou canst not see my face ; for there shall no man see me and live." (Ex. xxiii. 20.) And Paul speaks of him as one " whom no man hath seen, nor can see." (1 Tim. vi. 16.)

It is little that children will learn from the Bible concerning the origin of evil, when, against " I make peace and create evil. I the Lord do all these things;" (Is. xlv. 7.) " out of the mouth of the Most High proceedeth not evil and good?" (Lam. iii. 38.)—they set, " without note or comment," " God is not the author of confusion;" (1 Cor. xiv. 33.) " a God of truth, and without iniquity, just and right is he." (Deut. xxxii. 4.) " God cannot be tempted with evil, neither tempteth he any man." (Jas. i. 13.)

Concerning the divine dwelling-place, we read that " the Lord appeared to Solomon, and said . . . I have chosen and sanctified this house . . . and mine eyes and heart shall be there perpetually." (2 Chron. vii. 12-16.) Yet we also read, " Howbeit the Most High dwelleth not in temples made with hands." (Acts vii. 48.) In one place he is described as " dwelling in light which no man can approach;" (1 Tim. iv. 16.) and in another it is said, " clouds and darkness are round about him." (Ps. xcvii. 2.)

Similarly contrast these also: " The Lord is a man of war:" (Ex. xv. 3.) " The Lord mighty in battle:" (Ps. xxiv. 8.) " The Lord of hosts is his name." (Is. li. 15.) And, "God is not the author of confusion, but of peace." (1 Cor. xiv. 33.) " Bloody men shall not live out half their days." (Ps. lv. 23.) " The God of peace be with you all." (Rom. xv. 33.)

In reference to the making and worshipping of images, we have the positive command, " Thou shalt not make unto thee any graven image, or any likeness of anything that is in heaven above, or in the earth beneath. Thou shalt not bow down to them, nor serve (or worship) them," (Ex. xxii. 4.) and many repeated denunciations of idolatry. Yet Moses was commanded to " make two

cherubim of gold." (xxv. 18.) Also, "the Lord said
unto Moses, make thee a fiery serpent, and set it upon a
pole, and it shall come to pass that every one that is
bitten, when he looketh upon it, shall live." (Num. xxi. 8.)
A direct act of idolatry commanded by God himself!

The books of Exodus and Leviticus abound in directions instituting and regulating sacrifice, in terms such
as "Thou shalt offer every day a bullock for a sin-offering
for atonement;" (Ex. xxix. 36; also xviii.; Lev. i. 9;
xxiii. 27, &c.) and the most complex and gorgeous
system of ceremonial worship was based upon it, expressly by divine command. Yet in the Psalms we find
the Almighty exclaiming, "Will I eat the flesh of bulls,
or drink the blood of goats? Offer unto God thanks-
giving, and pay thy vows unto the Most High." (Ps. l.
13, 14.) And in Isaiah, "To what purpose is the mul-
titude of your sacrifices unto me? saith the Lord . . .
I delight not in the blood of bullocks, or of lambs, or of
he-goats . . . When ye come to appear before me, who
hath required this at your hand? Bring no more vain
oblations; incense is an abomination unto me; the new
moons and Sabbaths, the calling of assemblies, I cannot
away with; it is iniquity, even the solemn meeting."
(Is. i. 11-13.) And Jeremiah represents the Almighty
as positively repudiating any connection with the Levi-
tical code. "I spake not unto your fathers, nor commanded them in the day that I brought them out of the
land of Egypt, concerning burnt-offerings or sacrifices."
(Gen. vii. 22.)

"Without note or comment," children would assuredly
fail to comprehend the significance of the antagonism
necessarily existing between the whole sacerdotal
class, with its "trivial round" of ritual and observance,

and immoral doctrine of compensation for moral deficiencies by material payments, and the honest, outspoken prophet or teacher of practical religion. And to fail to comprehend this, is to fail to learn one of the most valuable lessons to be derived from the Bible.

Even the horrible practice of human sacrifice finds justification with the sacerdotal followers of the Jewish divinity. We have already seen how, backed by the priests, David delivered up the seven sons and grandsons of Saul, "and they hanged them in the hill before the Lord . . . and after that God was entreated for the land." (2 Sam. xxi.) Moreover, "God said unto Abraham, take now thy son, thine only son Isaac . . . and offer him for a burnt-offering." (Gen. xxii. 2.) Jephthah, too, "vowed a vow unto the Lord" that he would "offer up for a burnt-offering" whatever he met first on his return home, provided the Lord would give him a victory. The victory was given, and the bargain was kept; "the Lord," of course, being in his omniprescience, well aware what it involved; and, to judge by his antecedent and subsequent conduct, by no means incapable of being induced thereto by the magnitude of the bribe. Jephthah's own daughter was the first to come to congratulate her father; "and he did with her according to his vow." (Jud. xi.) The sacerdotal law gave him no choice, for it positively enacted that vows, however iniquitous, were not to be broken, except when taken under certain circumstances by a maid, a wife, or a widow. (Num. xxx.)

The liberality and mercifulness of God find expression in many touching declarations in the Scriptures. We read that "every one that asketh, receiveth, and he that seeketh, findeth." (Matt. vii. 8.) "Those that seek me early shall find me." (Prov. viii. 17.) Yet on the other side we have, "Then shall they call upon me, but I will not answer; they shall seek me early, but they shall not find me." (i. 28.) And notwithstanding such assertions as: "The Lord is very pitiful and of tender mercy." (James v. 11.) "He doth not afflict willingly, nor grieve the children of men." (Lam. iii. 33.) "The Lord is good to all, and his tender mercies are over all his works." (Ps. cxlv. 9.) "I have no pleasure in the death of him that dieth, saith the Lord God." (Ezek. xviii. 32.) "God is love;" (1 John iv. 16.) "Who will have all men to be saved;" (1 Tim. ii. 4.) "For his mercy endureth for ever:" (1 Chron. xvi. 34, &c.)—we find also the following ferocious utterances: "The Lord thy God is a consuming fire." (Deut. iv. 34.) "I will dash them one against another, even the fathers and the sons together, saith the the Lord. I will not pity, nor spare, nor have mercy, but destroy them." (Jer. xiii. 14.) "And thou shalt consume all the people which the Lord thy God shall deliver thee: thine eye shall have no pity upon them." (Deut. vii. 16, and 2.) "Thus saith the Lord of hosts . . . slay both man and woman, infant and suckling, ox and sheep, camel and ass." (1 Sam. xv. 2, 3.) "Because they had looked into the ark of the Lord, even he smote of the people fifty thousand and threescore and ten men. And the people lamented because the Lord had smitten many of the people with great slaughter." (1 Sam. vi. 19.) "I also will deal in fury; mine eye shall not spare, neither will I have pity. And though they cry in mine ears with a loud voice, yet will I not hear them." (Ezek. viii. 18.) "And the Lord said, Go through the city and smite; let not your eye spare, neither have ye pity: slay utterly old and young, both maids and little children, and women. . . . and begin at my sanctuary." (ix. 4-6.)

It is no less impossible to derive from the Bible alone any certainty of God's unfailing truthfulness than of his mercy. It is true that we are told, "It is impossible for God to lie." (Heb. vi. 18.) "Lying lips are an abomination to the Lord." (Prov. xii. 22.) "Thou shalt not bear false witness against thy neighbour." (Ex. xx. 16.) "These things doth the Lord hate . . . a lying tongue . . . a false witness that speaketh lies." (Prov. iv. 17-19.) And, "all liars shall have their part in the lake which burneth with fire and brimstone." (Rev. xxi. 8.) Yet, on the other hand, we find the lies of the Israelitish women in Egypt, and of Rahab in Jericho, justified;— "that admirable falsehood," as St. Chrysostom called the latter. (Ex. i. 18-20; Josh. ii. 4-6.) We find the atrocious deceit of Jael more than justified. (Jud. iv. v.) And we have also this astounding revelation from behind the scenes in heaven:—"And the Lord said, who shall persuade Ahab? . . . And there came forth a spirit and stood before the Lord, and said, I will persuade him. And the Lord said, wherewith? And he said, I will go forth and be a lying spirit in the mouth of all these thy prophets. And he said, thou shalt persuade him, and prevail also; go forth and do so. Now, therefore, behold the Lord hath put a lying spirit in the mouth of all these thy prophets, and the Lord hath spoken evil concerning thee." (1 Kings xxii. 21-23.) And in confirmation of this otherwise incredible narrative, we read later, "If the prophet be deceived when he hath spoken a thing, I the Lord have deceived that prophet, and I will stretch out mine hand upon him, and will destroy him from the midst of my people." (Ezek. xiv. 9.) The New Testament adopts a similar view of God's dealings; for, mingled with its "glad tidings of salvation," we read,—

"God shall send them strong delusion, that they should believe a lie, that they all might be damned." (2 Thess. ii. 11, 12.)

Once more it must be asked, Can we wonder that earnest and pious men of our own times have, in their zeal for the honour of God, endeavoured to rescue his character from the treatment it receives in the Scriptures?

VIII.

The character of Jesus is as variously drawn in the New Testament as that of the Deity in the Old; and those who desire the children in our schools to recognise in him the perfect man and infallible Teacher, should, to be consistent, be the very last to wish them to read the New Testament "without note or comment." Too often it happens that the explanatory lessons with which the Scriptures are accompanied, are utterly pernicious, and even blasphemous. This very year, a youth who has been for some years a student in one of the wealthiest of our public foundation-schools, was required to give some instances of human feeling on the part of Jesus. Of the value, whether intellectually or religiously, of the education given at that school, we may judge by his answer. Of the tender sympathy shown by Jesus towards all who were suffering; of his unselfish devotion to the cause of the poor and the depraved; of his noble indignation against injustice and oppression; of his intense sense of a personal Father in God, and instinctive detestation of all sacerdotal interference:—of all these so eminently human characteristics, our scholar said nothing. The result of his compulsory attendance at the school chapel every morning, and at two full services every

Sunday, beside much other Scripture instruction, was to impress upon him the belief that whatever is human is bad, and whatever is bad is human. He concluded, therefore, that by human feeling on the part of Jesus, an instance of something bad was intended. And he actually sent up for answer, as a solitary instance of human feeling on the part of Jesus, the story of his losing his temper, and cursing a fig-tree for being barren when it was not the season for figs! (Mark xi. 13, 14, 21.)

As any explanations which accompany the reading of the Old Testament should be contrived to disabuse children of the notion that the Deity could ever have been such a being as is there described, so in reading of Jesus in the New Testament they should be told that there are indications of a better man than the Gospels make him, peeping out through the corrupted text. " It is impossible that such love and devotion as followed him throughout his life could ever have been won by a hard, unjust, or intolerant character." Yet he is represented as more than once addressing his admirable and devoted mother in a rough, unfilial tone; (John ii. 4; Luke ii. 4.) and launching most uncalled for reproaches at a gentleman of whose hospitality he was partaking, on the occasion of a woman coming in and washing his feet with her tears, and wiping them with her hair. (Luke vii. 32-50.)

Nor can there be any doubt as to what must be their natural judgment of the spirit of one who could describe his own mission in these terms: " Whosoever shall confess me before men, him will I also confess before my Father which is in heaven. But whosoever will deny me before men, him will I also deny before my Father which is in heaven. Think not that I am come to send peace on earth: I come not to send peace, but a sword. For I am come to set a man at variance against his father, and the daughter against her mother, and the daughter-in-law against her mother-in-law, and a man's foes shall be they of his own household." (Matt. x. 32-36.) Hardly will they reconcile this with the promise of his birth-song, "On earth peace, good-will toward men;" (Luke ii. 14.) but will hastily conclude that the angels were sadly misinformed. And when they read that one who is elsewhere described as "going about teaching and healing" among a people who were "perishing for lack of knowledge," uttered to his disciples such words as these, "Unto you it is given to know the mysteries of the kingdom of God: but unto others in parables; that seeing they might not see, and hearing they might not understand;" (Luke viii. 8.) and read further, "Therefore they could not believe, because he hath blinded their eyes and hardened their heart; that they should not see with their eyes, nor understand with their heart, and be converted, and I should heal them;" (John xii. 39, 40.)—and from these fearful utterances, turn to the declaration, that this same Jesus had received "all power in heaven and earth;" (Matt. xxviii. 18.) and that he "came not to judge but to save the world;" (John xii. 27.) came especially "to seek and to save that which was lost;" (Luke xix. 10.) it will be no wonder if their souls finally succumb to despair, and they cry to their teachers, "Be merciful: take away from us this book, if you dare not explain to us its meaning."

IX.

I shall conclude the present lecture by pointing out the notable contradiction apparent between the Bible and the fact of the world's present existence. The New Testament contains scarcely a passage of any length that does not make some allusion to the near approach of the end of the world.

We may conceive the perplexity of children when, after reading in ordinary history the events of the last eighteen hundred years, with their piteous tale of cruelty and oppression, disease and death, they open their Bibles and read that, all those centuries ago, men were summoned to repent because "the kingdom of heaven" was then "at hand;" (Matt. iv. 17.) and find that by "the kingdom of heaven" was meant, not merely a social or moral regeneration, though the phrase is sometimes used in this sense, but the personal second coming of Christ, and end of all things. That both the Baptist and Jesus preached thus: that the twelve apostles were sent forth to preach thus; (x. 7.) that the seventy were charged with injunctions to announce to the inhabitants of any city on their entry, "the kingdom of God is come nigh unto you;" (Luke x. 8-11.) that Jesus represented himself as a nobleman who had gone into a far country to receive for himself a kingdom, and to return; and instructed his disciples in these terms, "Occupy till I come;" (xix. 13.) that this was the kingdom for which Joseph of Arimathea "waited;" (xxiii. 51.) unto which Paul prayed that he might be preserved; (2 Tim. iv. 18.) charging Timothy to "keep the commandment. . . . . until the appearance of our Lord Jesus Christ." (1 Tim. vi. 14.)

How bewildering to the youthful intelligence, to perceive the world still going on much in its old track, slowly elaborating its own destiny, and to find in the records of its history no trace of the dread phenomena which they read in their Testaments were to portend and accompany the return of the Son of Man and of God,—the darkened sun, the falling stars, the bloodshot moon, the roaring sea, the myriad hosts of heaven, the voice of the archangel, and the trump of God; the judgment of the quick and dead, the wailing of the lost, and the gathering of the elect from the four winds of heaven, the resurrection of those who slept, the ecstasy of "we who remain," as Paul said, (1 Thess. iv. 15-17.) when "caught up to meet the Lord in the air," on his "coming in the clouds of heaven with power and great glory;" (Matt. xxiv. 29-35.) for which all the disciples were bid to watch; (Mark xiii. 37.) and which some of them were still to be alive on earth to see. For Jesus had said, "Verily I say unto you, that there be some of them that stand here now which shall not taste of death till they have seen the kingdom of God come with power." (Matt. xvi. 28; Mark xi. 1; Luke xix. 27.) "*Immediately* after the tribulation of those days:" and, "Verily I say unto you, this generation shall not pass away, until all these things shall be fulfilled." (Matt. xxiv. 29, 35.) Add, too, the assurance of the angels to the disciples as they stood watching the Ascension, that he should return "in like manner;" (Acts i. 11.) add the declaration of Peter that "the end of all things is at hand;" (1 Pet. iv. 7.) add the admonition of Paul to the Romans, "Now it is high time to awake out of sleep, for now is our salvation nearer than when we believed. The night is far spent, the day is at hand;" (Rom. xiii. 11, 12.) "these last days;" (Heb. i. 2.) even the days of us "upon whom the ends of the world are come;" (1 Cor. x. 11.) add, lastly, the final book of "The Revelation," opening with the announcement that these things "must shortly come to pass ;" and concluding with the declaration, "Surely I come quickly. Amen. Even so, come, Lord Jesus,"—a book which, claiming to be the final utterance of divine truth, is charged with dire curses against any who should add to it; instead of saying, rather, " to be continued, so long as God continues to work in man,"—add, I say, to all that has been set forth, these and the yet other numerous similar intimations of the then expected rapidly approaching end ; set children to read them " without note or comment," but with the belief which they will inevitably acquire, from the fact of the Bible being put into their hands without information to the contrary,—the belief that it must therefore be all infallibly true, that God *did* speak, the Lord *did* say, all the things therein ascribed to him ; and then, if they retain any particle of intelligence whatever, most surely they will have but a confused idea of God, a confused idea of man, and a confused idea of the relations between them ; a confused idea of right and wrong, a confused idea of faith and fact ; or rather, we may confidently declare, a false and pernicious idea of all things whatsoever, in heaven and earth, from beginning to end.

LECTURE THE SECOND.

X.

It is not unusual for people, when pressed upon the subject, to say, "We do not lay much store by the Old Testament. We concede much of what you say against it as a teacher of morality and even of religion. We value it chiefly as the basis and introduction of the New. It is upon the New Testament that we take our stand. The sufficient, and only sufficient, rule of life, its practical religion and morality, are distinct and unimpeachable." I propose, therefore, to conclude my examination of the effects of the popular proposition, "that the Bible be read without note or comment," by showing that in respect of its teaching, both religious and moral, even the New Testament requires elucidation and correction to prevent it from being productive of much that would be immoral, irreligious, and grossly superstitious.

Passing over the innumerable discrepancies in the gospel narratives, to reconcile which so many "Harmonies" have been constructed in vain, let us compare first those utterances of the New Testament which have regard to life—civil, political, and social. Are our children to learn from its pages to grow up to be intelligent and independent citizens, respecting the laws, and respecting themselves? It is clear that, "without note or comment," they will hardly escape great perplexity of conscience when on one side they read, "Be subject to principalities and powers, obey magistrates." (Tit. iii. 1.) "Obey them that have the rule over you, and submit yourselves." (Heb. xiii. 17.) "The powers that be are ordained of God. Whoso therefore resisteth the power, resisteth the ordinance of God:" (Rom. xiii. 1, 2.) and on the other side, find, that no sooner did a dilemma arise, than "Peter and the other apostles answered and said, We ought to obey God rather than man." (Acts v. 29.)

Concerning the institution of Slavery, we find in the Old Testament the most conflicting utterances, of which one is, "Of the children of the strangers that do sojourn among you, of them shall ye buy . . . and they shall be your possession. . . . They shall be your bondmen for ever:" (Lev. xxv. 45, 46.) and another, "Thou shalt neither vex a stranger nor oppress him;" (Ex. xxxii. 21.) both of which are in the books ascribed to Moses. While the New Testament contains no direct reprobation of Slavery, but rather the reverse. It must be remembered that, wherever in our translation the word *servant* occurs, the original means *slave*. And while masters are enjoined to "give unto their slaves that which is just and equal" for their labour, and to "forbear threatening" them; (Col. iv. 1; Eph. vi. 9.) it says nothing in repudiation of the institution itself as being unjust and unequal; but repeatedly admonishes slaves to be content with their condition; to "count their masters worthy of all honour;" (1 Tim. vi. 1.) and be "obedient to them with fear and trembling." (Eph. vi. 5.) We read, moreover, that Paul himself sent back to his master the slave Onesimus, after converting him to Christianity. (Philemon.)

There are, indeed, ample grounds for fearing lest all respect for Rights vanish in the prominence given exclusively to Duties. And even in the important matter of respect and affection for parents and relatives, children may fail to find a sufficient rule to exclude hesitation. It is true that they read, "Honour thy father and mother," for the low and unsatisfactory motive, "that thy days may be long." (Ex. xx. 12.) " Husbands love your wives." (Eph. v. 25.) And "whoso hateth his brother is a murderer." (1 John iii. 15.) But there is to be set on the other side this of Jesus himself, " If any man hate not his father, and mother, and wife, and children, and brethren, and sisters . . . he cannot be my disciple." (Luke xiv. 26.)

Great will be their perplexity, too, when, after the ordinary lessons of the schoolroom, inculcating respect for property, the duty of industry, forethought, and thrift, the disgrace of beggary, and evil of pauperism, they read " without note or comment," " Take therefore no thought for the morrow ;" "Lay not up for yourselves treasures upon earth."(Matt. vi. 34, 19.) "Sell whatsoever thou hast and give to the poor ;" (Mark x. 21.) and see how Jesus backed up his communistic precepts by his practice, in instituting the order of Mendicant Friars, by sending forth the Twelve and the Seventy with injunctions to " carry neither purse nor scrip." (Luke x. 3-7, &c.)

Neither can we consistently endeavour to cherish in children a love of science, literature, and art, and all the glorious uses of which man's high faculties are capable ; a love, in short, of that mental culture to obtain which we expressly send them to school ; if we ply them with such contemptuous allusions to it as " Beware lest any man spoil you with philosophy and vain deceit ; " (Col.

ii. 8.) "The Greeks seek after wisdom ;" (1 Cor. i. 22.) "Vain babblings and oppositions of science falsely so called ;" (1 Tim. vi. 20.) "Knowledge puffeth up ;" (1 Cor. viii. 1.)—without telling them at the same time, that ignorance ever "puffeth up" far more than knowledge; that "science," now-a-days stands on a very different basis to that on which it stood in those days, namely, on a basis of positive fact as ascertained by actual investigation into the phenomena of the universe, instead of on the imaginations and foregone conclusions of men who believed in the infallibility of their mental impressions, and pretended to knowledge independently of experience ; and that it is our highest duty and privilege to cultivate "every good gift and every perfect gift," intellectual and other, "which cometh down from the Father of lights." (Jam. i. 17.)

Even in so simple a matter as the advantage of bearing a good character, they will be at a loss to determine between "a good name is better than precious ointment ;" (Eccl. vii. 1.) "it is rather to be chosen than great riches ;" (Prov. xxii. 1.) and, "Woe unto you when all men shall speak well of you." (Luke vi. 25.)

The Bible makes it a reproach to King Asa that "in his disease he sought not to the Lord, but to the physicians," and significantly adds, "Asa slept with his fathers." (2 Chron. xvi. 12.) Of another patient it is said that she had "for twelve years suffered many things of many physicians, and had spent all that she had, and was nothing bettered, but rather grew worse," but straightway was healed through faith. (Mark v. 25-29.) And there is this express injunction, "Is any sick among you? let him call for the elders of the Church, and let them pray over him, anointing him with oil in the name of the

Lord: and the prayer of faith shall save the sick, and the Lord shall raise him up." (Jam. v. 14.) "Without note or comment," but influenced, unconsciously perhaps, within school or without it, to regard the plain teaching of the Bible as intended to be followed unshrinkingly, the children in our National Schools will be apt to grow up with the belief that it is unchristian and wicked to call in a doctor, or to take medicine, when they are ill.

Lawyers are scarcely named but to be censured in such terms as these: "Woe unto you lawyers! for ye lade men with burdens grievous to be borne, and ye yourselves touch not the burdens with one of your fingers. Woe unto you lawyers!" (Luke xi. 45, 52.) For "without note or comment," the term rendered "lawyers," will inevitably be held to signify, not the expounders of Rabbinical doctrine, but the members of that eminent profession which is so indispensable to the maintenance of our rights and privileges. While the despised "publicans" of Jewish times, instead of being recognised as mere collectors of taxes, are sure to be confounded with our own respectable company of "licensed victuallers."

We have seen how summarily two of the learned professions may be disposed of. Following the Bible without guidance by "note or comment," the clergy will be in danger of faring little better than the lawyers or doctors. And this brings us to the subject of religious duties as laid down in the New Testament.

It is, whether rightly or wrongly I do not venture to decide, a subject of peculiar pride with us, that we are a prayerful and churchgoing people. But what is really curious is, that the practice of assembling together for public worship, we regard as essential to our character as *Christians*. Now, how can children be expected to understand "without note or comment" that it is their duty to attend "divine service," when they find that Jesus, who is held up to them as the infallible pattern and guide of life, never joined in public prayer himself, but always when he wished to pray or meditate went apart, either "up into a mountain," (Matt. xiv. 23.) or some other "solitary place," (Mark i. 35.) or "withdrew about a stone's cast;" (Luke xxii. 24.) that he only went into the synagogue or the temple to read or to teach; (Luke iv. 16: Matt. xxi. 23.) or to indulge in what to children and unexplained must appear to be riotous conduct in church, namely to drive out with blows and threats a number of persons who were exercising a lawful industry in its precincts; (Matt. xxi. 12.) that the persons he mentioned in one of his parables as "going up to the temple to pray," (Luke xviii. 10.) belonged to the classes he most persistently denounced, being a pharisee and a publican; and even these he distinctly exonerates from the reproach of having joined in *common* prayer; that moreover, in addition to his example, he delivered precepts absolutely prohibitory of all public praying in these emphatic terms: "When thou prayest, thou shalt not be as the hypocrites are; for they love to pray standing in the synagogues, and in the corners of the streets to be seen of men. Verily, I say unto you, They have their reward. But thou, when thou prayest, enter into thy closet, and when thou hast shut thy door, pray to thy Father which is in secret; and thy Father which seeth in secret, shall reward thee openly;" (Matt. vi. 5, 6.)—a rule which he relaxed only on the condition that two, or at most three, should agree upon a subject for petition, in which case they might gather together in his name. (Matt. xviii. 19, 20.) It is indeed a painful perplexity in which the minds of the more sensitive children will be plunged when they ask themselves how, in the face of Christ's most positive precepts and example, they can continue to pray in church or chapel, and at the same time deserve to be called by his name.

The propriety of continuing to observe the Sabbath, if rested on the Bible alone, will remain, to say the least, doubtful. The difference in the reasons assigned for its institution can hardly fail to create wonder as to the authority upon which the command said to be " written with the finger of God" himself, basing the appointment upon the creation of the universe in six days, (Ex. xxxi. 17, &c.) was changed to one representing it as a memorial of the deliverance out of Egypt. (Deut. v. 15.) While the institution itself is, on account of the abuses to which it led, referred to variously by the later prophets ; and, in the New Testament, seems to have been repudiated in a great measure, if not altogether, by Jesus and the apostles ; Paul distinctly admonishing the Colossians in these terms : " You hath Christ quickened. . . . blotting out the handwriting of ordinances. . . . Let no man therefore judge you . . . in respect of an holiday, . . . or of the Sabbath." (Col. ii. 13-16.) So that something at any rate has to be added to the New Testament to justify our present usage in this respect.

In the absence of explanatory comment, the statements of scripture respecting the resurrection of the body appear in direct conflict with each other; as also do those respecting the after-life of the soul. In the Old Testament we are told, "He that goeth down to the grave shall come up no more." (Job vii. 9.) "The dead know not anything, neither have they any more reward." (Eccl. ix. 5, 10.) And in the New Testament, "The trumpet shall sound, and the dead shall be raised ;" (1 Cor. xv. 52.)

"Then shall he reward every man according to his works." (Matt. xvi. 27.) While the narratives of the ascent of Enoch and Elijah seem to find a positive contradiction in the declaration of Jesus, "No man hath ascended up to heaven but he that came down from heaven, even the son of man;" and the narrative makes him add, "which is in heaven," putting what appears to be an absurd contradiction into the mouth of Jesus. (John iii. 12.)

And even concerning the status of Jesus himself, explanations are needed to reconcile the various contradictory declarations; "I and my Father are one." (John x. 30.) "He thought it not robbery to be equal with God." (Phil. ii. 6.) "Jesus increased in wisdom and stature, and in favour with God and man." (Luke ii. 52.) "My Father is greater than I." (John xiv. 28.) "Of that day and that hour knoweth no man. . . Neither the Son, but the Father." (Mark xiii. 32.) And his agonised exclamation when dying, which we can easily believe to have been held up by the clergy of those days as uttered in remorse of soul for a life spent in opposition to the church orthodoxy of his country,—"My God, my God, why hast thou forsaken me?" (Matt. xxvii. 46.)

XI.

Much stress has been laid by orthodox writers on the "Continuity," or uninterrupted connection, of Scripture. The inference which they have drawn from the consistency existing between its various parts, is that it must all be alike the result of one divine harmonious scheme. That such Continuity exists it is impossible to help seeing, but the extent to which it exists, and its significance in relation to what is called doctrinal religion, are likely, " without note or comment," wholly to escape the observation of youthful scholars.

The whole religious system of the Old Testament rests upon the theory that the object of Religion is, not the exaltation of man, but the delectation of the Deity ; and the stimulants offered in it to the practice of religion are of the most material and seductive kind, wealth, honour, long life, numerous posterity. In the New Testament the same idea is continued, with this difference, that experience having demonstrated the theory to be unsound as regards this life, inasmuch as prosperity does not by any means always accompany virtue, nor adversity vice, rewards and punishments are there reserved for a future state of existence, in a region inaccessible to verification by experience.

Two other instances of Continuity between the two divisions of Scripture may be classed together as being intimately connected with each other. These are, the institution of Sacrifice, and the character of the Jewish Deity. To the instances already given of the amazing ferocity of this Being, as represented in the Sacred Books of the Jews, may be added the tremendous threats and penalties denounced for the smallest transgressions, the readiness to dart forth from the mountain and deal destruction upon any who might but touch it ; and the perpetual demand for blood. This propensity for blood constitutes a notable instance of Continuity in the character of the God of the Bible. Blood of animals; blood of peoples hostile to the Israelites ; blood of transgressors among the Israelites ; and in numerous instances, blood of unoffending men, women, and children, even from among his own chosen people.

(1 Sam. vi. 19; 2 Sam. xxiv. 15; Ezek. ix. 6; &c.) We have already dealt with David's sacrifice of the seven sons of Saul: "They hanged them in the hill before the Lord. . . . and after that God was entreated for the land;" (2 Sam. xxi.) Jephthah's sacrifice of his daughter; (Jud. xi.) and Abraham's attempt to sacrifice his son. (Gen. xxii.) Of this last I must speak more fully, because there are, holding high positions both in the church and in popular estimation, as thinkers and scholars, men who insist on drawing from it a moral which they deem favourable to the character of the deity as represented in the Jewish Scriptures. But at present they have failed to do more than read back into the Bible the civilisation of their age and their own personal amiability. So far from their being justified in regarding the arrest of Abraham as a protest on the part of the Deity against the prevailing custom of human sacrifices, the narrative distinctly asserts that "God tempted Abraham" to commit the horrid deed: that *his consent to commit it* was accepted at the time as an "act of faith," and rewarded by a renewal of the promise of a numerous posterity; and not only is there in the Scriptures no expression whatever commending him for refraining from completing the sacrifice, but the New Testament treats it approvingly as being as good as completed, saying in one place, "By faith Abraham, when he was tried, *offered up* Isaac; and he that had received the promises *offered up* his only-begotten son;" (Heb. xi. 17.) and in another place, "Was not Abraham our father justified by works, when he *had offered* Isaac his son upon the altar? Seest thou how faith wrought with his works, and by works faith was made perfect?" (Jam. ii. 21, 22.)

So far from the principle of human sacrifices, or the belief in a deity who required to be propitiated by blood, being repudiated in the New Testament, "the Continuity of Scripture" is in these respects plain and indisputable, and the principle is carried to a height undreamt of in Old Testament times. The God of the Jewish priests requires at length the blood of his own "only-begotten," "beloved" son! It is only when this tremendous climax has been reached that the dread thirst is appeased. This is the fundamental argument of the eminently sacerdotal epistle to the Hebrews, (of unknown authorship). In it we are assured that "without shedding of blood there is no remission of sins." (Heb. ix. 22.) A human parent, not in this respect "made in the image of God," can forgive a repenting errant child. The divine parent, made by priests, and at once unhuman and inhuman, must have his "pound of flesh" from somebody. This epistle tells us concerning Christ that " neither by the blood of goats and calves, but by his own blood he entered in once into the holy place, having obtained eternal redemption for us. . . . . So Christ was once offered to bear the sins of many;" (ix. 12, 28.) thus adopting and justifying the view of the high-priest Caiaphas, who, by virtue of his sacerdotal office, counselled and "prophesied that Jesus should die for the people;" (John xi. 50, 51.)—a view shared even by John himself, who in one of his epistles declares that "God sent his only begotten Son to be the propitiation for our sins." (1 John iv. 9, 10.) Thus early were the attempts of Jesus to abolish sacerdotalism, and promulgate purer notions of the Deity, defeated by his own disciples, or by those who wrote in their names; and the reformation which constituted the real Christianity, overlaid and stifled by "the Church."

Let the churches called Christian, demonstrate, if they will, their "Continuity" with the most hideous of Jewish superstitions; and cherish the recollection of the worst side of the Jewish Divinity, by perpetual repetitions of the rite which, while declining to practice it simply "in remembrance" of a loved and lost benefactor, they yet profanely style "the *holy* Eucharist." Say they, it requires a miracle to keep the church up? Well, perhaps it does. But if we who "have not so learned Christ" are to act consistently with our more advanced ideas of religion and morality, the "notes and comments" by which the reading of these passages in our schools is accompanied, must direct attention rather to the higher and better teaching of prophetical lips; "the sacrifices of God are a contrite heart;" (Ps. li. 17.) "he saveth such as be of a contrite spirit;" (xxxiv. 18.) and "dwelleth with him that is of a contrite and humble spirit;" (Is. lvii. 15.) as well as that of Jesus himself, "If a man love me he will keep my words; and my Father will love him, and we will come unto him, and make our abode with him." (John xiv. 23.) There is no savour of blood here.

If an education is to be imparted that is consistent with "the development of the intellect and moral sense," the doctrine that justice can be satisfied by the substitution of the innocent for the guilty, must be rigidly excluded from our schools. It is true that this doctrine is not without a certain significance; that there is a way by which the position of the wicked may be bettered through the condemnation of the righteous. For the punishment of the innocent involves the divine law of justice being, not fulfilled, but so utterly shattered and destroyed, as to be thenceforth absolutely non-existent. The sinner's gain, therefore, would consist in there being no law of justice by which he could be arraigned.

But so invincibly implacable is the deity of at least a great portion of the New Testament, that even such stupendous atonement fails to gain him over. Its benefits are confined to a fortunate few, and his fury towards the rest is redoubled. As Burns says, he

> "Sends ane to heaven, and ten to hell
> A' for his glory."

The penalties of evil-doing are infinitely enhanced, and they are applied to a fresh class of offences. Here, too, Continuity is combined with progression; but it is, morally, a progression backwards. The Old Testament consigns no one to eternal punishment, neither does it make penal the conclusions of the intellect. The New Testament abounds in menaces of the most fearful character, not only against malefactors, but also against unbelievers. It represents the Almighty, when punishing the reprobate, as uninfluenced by anything analogous to the human motive of promoting the security of society or the reformation of the criminal, but inflicting torture in the spirit of a fiend, out of pure malignity, because with no advantage to any. "The unbelieving and the abominable" are classed together, and, we read, "shall have their part in the lake which burneth with fire and brimstone;" (Rev. xxi. 8.) "where their worm dieth not, and the fire is not quenched;" (Mark ix. 44.) "there shall be weeping and gnashing of teeth." (Matt. viii. 12.) "Depart ye cursed," is the final doom of those who had failed to recognise Christ on earth, "depart ye cursed into everlasting fire, prepared for the devil and his angels." (Matt. xxv. 41.)

Nay, more than this. The gospels, as we have them, actually represent Jesus himself as pronouncing sentence of damnation upon all who cannot work miracles. His last words to his disciples are thus reported: "Go ye into all the world, and preach the gospel to every creature. . . He that believeth not shall be damned. And these signs shall follow them that believe: in my name they shall cast out devils; they shall speak with new tongues; they shall take up serpents; and if they drink any deadly thing it shall not hurt them; they shall lay hands on the sick, and they shall recover." (Mark xiv. 16.) Not to work miracles is not to believe, and not to believe is to be damned. Is it not certain that if the young are allowed to read the New Testament without explanation or correction by "note or comment," they will, as have millions of tender souls to their inexpressible terror and anguish, find the gospel of Jesus to be to them but a gospel of damnation?

Let us return to this world and the practical concerns of life. In its manner of dealing with the crucial act of life, marriage, and its treatment of the relations of the sexes generally, the New Testament takes, in regard to the Old, a great step backwards. A demonstration of its vacillation and utter inadequacy to provide rules for the conduct of civilised life on this most important of all points connected with morals, will fitly conclude this division of the subject. To the commendation of impotency uttered by Jesus, the stress laid by him upon mere physical fidelity, (Matt. xix. 9, 12.) and his disregard of all incongruity or incompatibility of character or affection, as a plea for separation, (a peculiarity which we have in our institutions but too faithfully followed), must be added these sentences of Paul: "Art thou bound to a wife? Seek not to be loosed. Art thou loosed from a wife? Seek not to be bound. . . It is better to marry than to burn," and, "good for the present distress." (1 Cor. vii. 27, 9, 29.) Hardly from this will our youth learn to recognise love as capable of being a pure and an elevating influence, or to give to Christianity the credit, so often claimed for it, of having raised woman from the depressed position in which that age found her. It will be in vain that they read "Marriage is honourable in all," (Heb. xiii. 4.) when they find the prevailing spirit of the gospel to be ascetic, exalting absolute chastity as one of the loftiest of virtues, and denouncing all natural desire as sinful in itself. (1 Cor. vii. 1, 38; Rev. xiv. 4.) Will not the later teaching of Scripture appear to them to have receded sadly in its fitness for humanity, from the earlier which commanded men to "increase and multiply;" (Gen. i. 28.) commended a virtuous woman as "a crown to her husband;" (Prov. xii. 4.) and pronounced a blessing on "children and the fruit of the womb;" (Ps. cxxvii. 3, &c.) and, in so far as the relations of the sexes are concerned, excite in them a preference for the Jewish regime over the Christian?

The number is beyond all reckoning, of women, the best and noblest of their sex, the most fitted to be the mothers and early trainers of mankind, who through a superstitious regard to this characteristic of the New Testament, have renounced their natural "high calling," leaving to inferior types the fulfilment of the functions upon the right exercise of which the progress, elevation, and happiness of mankind depend; who have withdrawn themselves from the duties of real life into artificial isolation, through a conscientious but mistaken belief, that in practising the selfishness of the devotee, they are seeking a virtue which is possible only through the exercise of the affections. It is in vain that Paul in his riper experience wrote, "I will that the younger women marry, bear children, guide the house," (1 Tim. v. 14.) when Churches persist in making so much of his earlier utterance delivered, as he himself acknowledges, with hesitation and doubt. "The unmarried woman careth for the things of the Lord, that she may be holy both in body and spirit: but she that is married careth for the things of the world, how she may please her husband," and . . . "I *think* that I have the spirit of God," (1 Cor. vii. 34, 40.)—as if the best, the only way of serving God was not by serving man. This is but an expression and echo of that same Manichaean principle of Asceticism, which has led alike Pagans and Christians innumerable to despise the material world. Blasphemously divorcing the Creator from his work, it teaches that nature is so utterly corrupt and wrong, that the more we go against and mortify it, the more likely we are to be pure and right.

'And so it comes that woman, while promoted theologically to be "Queen of Heaven" and "Mother of God," ecclesiastically is regarded as a mistake of nature, a thing to be snubbed and repressed, and condemned to the living death of an enforced celibacy.'

One whom I dare to call the greatest of our philosophers, Herbert Spencer, has epitomised in a single sentence all that can be said on this subject:—"Morality is essentially one with physical truth. It is a kind of transcendental physiology." ("Social Statics.") It is through ignorance of this, the real basis and nature of morality, that myriads of the best women in Christendom have, in every generation, to the incalculable loss of the whole species, made the saddest shipwreck both of their own lives and of the lives which by their sweet and holy influence they might have rendered supremely blest.

There is a "Higher Law" of morality which impels us to suppress our own affections and desires, not through hope of reward here or hereafter; not through deference to conventional standards, but solely through an unselfish regard to the feelings of those to whom it is our lot to be allied. But that such a law is to be the law of our lives, and sole standard of virtue, we find no intimation in the Testament, Old or New.

XII.

Yet, notwithstanding the failure of the Bible to provide an authoritative or satisfactory rule either of morals or of religion, I hold that, both for its own intrinsic merits, and for the place which it occupies in the literature and history of ourselves and of mankind, it ought not to be excluded from the educational course of our children.

It was proposed in the London School-board to exclude it on the ground that its use as a religious text-book outside the schools, makes its admission into the schools inconsistent with religious equality. It certainly would be, as is generally allowed, an act of gross unfairness to admit partisan theology into a common school. But, happily, as is also very generally allowed, speculative dogma and practical religion are very far indeed from being one and the same thing; and even those who object most strongly to dogma in itself, desire to see children brought up religiously, that is with reverential regard for divine truth and law.

If fairness and impartiality forbid the Bible to be introduced and used as the text-book of any party or sect, they equally forbid it to be excluded for happening to be such a text-book. For this would equally constitute dogmatic teaching, though of a negative kind. Perfect fairness requires that the question of the introduction and use of a book within the schools, should not be in any way dependent upon dogmatic opinions entertained respecting it by parties outside the schools. Perfect fairness forbids that anything which is good and instructive in itself, be excluded merely on account of the source from which it is derived; be it from Turk, Infidel, Heretic, Pagan, Jew, or Christian. It is here that the limitation imposed by our definition of education, comes to our aid, " The cultivation of the intelligence and moral sense" by means of " whatsoever things are true, pure, and honest;" " that fear God, and work righteousness;" and are "profitable for doctrine (or teaching), for reproof, for correction, for instruction in righteousness."

Thus, in the common schools, nothing must be taught as being the " Word of God," or as *not* being the " Word of God:" either assertion being equally dogmatic. But everything must be allowed to derive its force from its own intrinsic character. And those who hold that the children ought to be taught to regard the Bible as being, or containing, exclusively the " Word of God," will only betray their own want of faith if they express misgivings lest that word fail to assert its own efficacy and speak its own divine message to the soul, without special enforcement as such by the schoolmaster.

Perhaps, too, upon the idea being put before them, they will even acquiesce in the suggestion, that for any man, be he schoolmaster or priest, or any body of men, lay or cleric, ancient or modern, even though dignified by the title of " General Council," to take upon themselves the responsibility of determining or declaring what is, or what is not, "the Word of God," is to lay themselves open to the charge of the most stupendous presumption of which finite being can possibly be guilty: a presumption which is no other than that of declaring themselves to be infallible, and entitled to sit in the temple of God as if they were God. (2 Thess. ii. 4.)

And further, to declare that the Bible is or contains exclusively "the Word of God," is to forbid the souls of men to find a divine message elsewhere than in the Bible. It is to dictate to God as well as to man. For it is to forbid God to make of others "ministers to do his will." (Ps. ciii. 21 ; Heb. i. 24.) It is to extract all meaning from the saying of Jesus, "Lo, I am with you alway, even unto the end of the world." (Matt. xxviii. 20.) It is to reject that "Spirit of truth" who was promised to "guide us into all truth." (John xvi. 13.) It is to "quench the Spirit that giveth life," in "the letter that killeth." (1 Thess. v. 1, 9 ; 2 Cor. iii. 6.) It is to insist that the Almighty speak to men, like a clergyman of the Establishment, only from a text in the Bible. Let us, if we will, define as "the Word of God" that which "feareth him and worketh righteousness ;" but let us not dogmatise as to what particular author or composition comes under that category. For "the Word of God" can only be the word or thought of which God makes use to impress the heart of any. If we "search the Scriptures," we find that neither by the writers of the Psalms, by the prophets, nor by Jesus, scarcely, if ever, is the phrase used to denote that which was already written, but only the deeper impression then present in the mind of the speaker or writer. If not used by God to impress the heart, it is then not "his word." The same utterance may be "his word" on one occasion, and not on another.

Varying for each person, it is not always the same for any person, inasmuch as that which impresses us in one mood, does not necessarily affect us in another. A "word of God" cannot fail, any more than a "law of God" can be broken. Any definition of Deity that does not exclude such a possibility, is an utterly inadequate definition, and one dishonouring to God.

But in the matter of the education of the young, we have to use our best judgment in apportioning the means to the end we have in view. And therefore we must put into their hands such reading only as is plainly adapted for their edification, whether we take it from the Bible or from any other book. It is for children to to be *in statu pupillari* to men. It is for men to be *in statu pupillari* to God.

I hold, then, that the Bible should be used in our common schools, First, for its intrinsic merits. In its pages we find the most complete revelation of humanity to be found in any written book, showing the gradual growth of the moral and spiritual faculties from the most rudimentary ages to the Christian era. We find this mainly in the exhibition of the rise and development, however irregular, of the *idea* of God, until, from a Being so limited in his nature and operations as to be able to sympathise and side with only a few individuals or a particular race, partaking all the deficiencies of their own gross, rude natures, bribed by gifts, appeased by sacrifices, partial, cruel, jealous, capricious, the patron and instigator of blood-thirsty and fraudulent men and actions, the resort and associate of "lying spirits," and sharing his sovereignty with the devil,—he is at length presented to us as "the high and holy one that inhabiteth eternity;" (Is. lviii. 15.) "the righteous judge;" (Rev.

xix. 11.) "creator of all things;" (Gen. i. 1, &c.) " Saviour of all men;" (1 Tim. iv. 10.) " whose kingdom ruleth over all." (Ps. ciii. 19).

Here we find first recorded the existence of a sense of responsibility for our actions to a law and a power which are above us. "Here human nature is drawn in all its extent, from its lowest depths to its loftiest reach; for the Bible is a gallery in which all the paintings are life-like, but the subjects so varied, that none are too gross for admission. Being a revelation of God according to the characters and imaginations of the men in whose consciousness his idea was conceived, it is emphatically a revelation of man, inasmuch as man's ideal is the index to his own character and degree of intelligence.

This, however, is no speciality of the Bible. It is the characteristic of all art and literature which speaks out the genuine deeper feelings of men's hearts; and in this respect, as containing the truest art, the Bible ranks as the highest classics.

In selecting from the world's literature, reading lessons inculcating "the true, the pure, and the lovely," who could have the heart to exclude the remarkable hymn of the creation; the significant allegory of Eden; the charming pastoral of Isaac and Rebekah in their first love; the touching idyl of Joseph and his brethren and their aged father; the wondrous romance of the Exodus; the story of Moses, that king of men; the noble recitations of law and legend in Deuteronomy; the interesting narratives of Samson, Samuel, David, and Solomon; the simple tales of Ruth and of Esther, so illustrative of the manners of the ancient east; the sublime poetry of Job and the Psalms; the shrewd wisdom of the Proverbs; the genial cynicism of Ecclesiastes; the magnificent outpourings of

Isaiah, denouncing the degradation and despair of his countrymen, and encouraging them anew to hope and to restoration through the moral regeneration of their nature? (Which of us even now could not point out some nation that has sore need of an Isaiah?) Then the noble lesson of Jonah, wherein children are oftener taught to see a tale of a cross-grained prophet, a whale, and a gourd, than to recognise the poet's protest against the popular notion, shared by Jonah, that the Lord was a mere district-god who could be avoided by change of place, and to see the moral of the fable in the representation of deity as everywhere present alike, even in the depths of the sea.

And, added to these, the exquisite purity and simplicity of the gospels, with their central figure of Jesus and his enthusiastic life-devotion to the cause of man's redemption from sin and suffering, and deliverance from the blighting effects of religious formalism, and the crushing weight of sacerdotalism; producing from the harmonious depths of his own great soul a sublime ideal of God as a Father, and a rule of life for man most noble in conception even when most impracticable of application. (Of all the characters of history, I know of none who would have sympathised more intensely with the object and the views I am seeking to advance, than the Christ whom I find in the gospels. Of course to the orthodox and the vested interests of his day, he was only a sad blasphemer and dangerous revolutionist.) Then, the varied and genuine humanity of the Epistles; and, notably, the magnificent monologue on charity, (in the thirteenth chapter of the first epistle to the Corinthians,) wherein Paul, dropping his too favourite character of Rabbinical lawyer and quibbling controversialist, soars to an altitude whither the churches have never yet been able to follow him. And, lastly, the lofty rhapsody of the Apocalypse, wherein fervid imagination, escaping from the woes beneath which mankind was being crushed by a Domitian and a Nero, took refuge in an ideal "state of God," where all wrongs should be redressed, all tears wiped away, the tormentors relegated to everlasting punishment, and sorrow and pain be no more for their victims.

And not for its intrinsic merits only, but for its influence on the hearts of mankind, should our children not be strangers to the volume in which, to borrow words from one of our most highly inspired writers, "book after book, law and truth and example, oracle and lovely hymn, and choral song of ten thousand thousand, and accepted prayers of saints and prophets, sent back as it were from heaven, like doves to be let loose again with a new freight of spiritual joys and griefs and necessities; where the hungry have found food, the thirsty a living spring, the feeble a staff, and the victorious warfarer songs of welcome and strains of music: which for more than a thousand years has gone hand in hand with civilisation, . . . often leading the way. . . . a book which good and holy men, the best and wisest of mankind, the kingly spirits of history enthroned in the hearts of mighty nations, have borne witness to its influences, and declared to be beyond compare the most perfect instrument, the only adequate organ of humanity; the organ and instrument of all the gifts, powers, and tendencies, by which the individual is privileged to rise above himself."*

To exclude all knowledge of the Bible from our youth, would be to make a greater gap in the education of a

* S.T. Coleridge's "Confessions of an Inquiring Spirit."

Briton than to omit almost any calculable number of other books, including the bulk of the world's history. Indeed it would be to exclude almost all history whatsoever; not ancient history merely, with knowledge of Egypt, Palestine, Syria, and Rome in its decline and fall; but the history of all Christendom itself, with that of the Papacy and the Reformation, and the whole of our own struggles for and against liberty; (for even we have not always been consistently on the side of freedom :) almost all of which struggles have been associated more or less with the Bible; the rise and origin, too, of the United States of America. All these in the past, together with our own condition in the present and hopes in the future, and the signification of the vast bulk of our literature, would, without some knowledge of the book that has filled a leading part in them all, be absolutely dark and meaningless.

Besides, there is not so much wisdom and beauty in the world that we can afford to throw any away. If we exclude the Bible altogether as being a text-book of our own religious sects, there is no plea upon which we can admit the admirable teaching that is to be found in the sacred books of the Hindoos and Chinese, the Mohammedans and Buddhists. Nay, to exclude the good parts of any book merely because it happens to be the text-book of a sect, is to put it in the power of any small knot of persons to secure the exclusion of any book whatsoever, by claiming it as one of their sacred books. Fancy a sect of Shakespeare worshippers getting by such means all knowledge of Shakespeare excluded from our educational course! Or a new sect of Pythagoreans to revive the worship of *numbers*, and, setting up Colenso as their high-priest, forcing us to exclude arithmetic from our schools!

Indeed, if only because of the very power and popularity of the Bible, it should not be left to be dealt with exclusively by a class of interpreters who acknowledge other allegiance than to the developed intellect and conscience of men. But, containing as it does, the whole sacred literature of the most remarkable of all ancient peoples, the Jews, and that of their most remarkable sect of religious reformers, the Christians, who, together, more than any other people, have influenced the development of the human mind and the course of human history; to exclude all knowledge of it from our youth would be to keep back from them the master-key to the heart and facts of humanity.

XIII.

But the fact of the Bible being, not a single book, but a whole literature ranging over many centuries, greatly simplifies the question of dealing with it. We rarely use the whole of any book in the schoolroom; never an entire literature. Imagine the whole, or samples of the whole, of our own literature being put at once into the hands of a child, with its rude early legends and ballads, its laws and statutes, its medicine and science, its trials and police-reports, and all the revolting details which even the least respectable of our newspapers suppress as "unfit for publication!" Yet this is what we have done with the ancient literature of the Jews. Instead of exercising any discrimination, we crowd our houses with it, we read it aloud to our families, we put it entire into the hands of our children; and when we find impurity and superstition rife among us, instead of admitting that we have done our best to promote them, we postulate the horrible doctrines of "original sin" and "total depravity," and shift the responsibility from our own shoulders to those of "the devil!" It was remarked once by a well-known Frenchman that "the English tolerate no indecencies except in their Bibles." Fatal exception, when we print Bibles in millions, in all the languages of the earth, and thrust them into the hands of every babe and suckling and growing youth.

The remedy which I propose is twofold: First, that a new version, omitting the whole of the parts which are objectionable on the score of decency, omitting also the headings by which ecclesiastical editors have sought to palliate immorality or strain the meaning to the support of particular doctrines, be made to take the place of the existing "authorised version;" and that this be done so completely that the old version be no longer accessible to the young, but continue to exist only as a curiosity or book of reference upon the shelves of students.

This change is one which, while it might be initiated by the School-boards undertaking to produce such a version for the use of their schools, would require both general and individual action on the part of the people themselves. It will be aided by the wise resolve of the Bible-revision Committee to omit the headings from their new and improved version. If the powers of this Committee were extended so as to enable it to make these changes, a great step towards carrying out this part of my proposed remedy would be gained. To further it would be an admirable occupation for a society which has existed for years among us under the presidency of Lord Shaftesbury, calling itself "The Pure Literature Society." Strange to say that, with all its zeal for purity in literature, it has never yet tried its hand on the Bible. It will indeed prove itself worthy of its high title and calling, when it joins in the chase of the "authorised version" from our homes, and the pews of our churches, so that children shall no longer be tempted to beguile the tedium of a sermon by feeding their curiosity on its improprieties.

It is related of Goëthe that he was present at a meeting of the Dutch clergy, when it was proposed to establish a censorship to enforce the expurgation of any improper books which might be brought forward for publication. Goëthe at once expressed his admiration of the plan, and recommended that they commence with the Bible. Whereupon the king of Holland said to him, " My dear Goëthe, pray hold your tongue. Of course you are quite right : but it won't do to say so."

This, however, is not enough. There are, as we have seen, very many portions of the Bible which, while not totally " unfit for publication," are yet shocking to the intellect and moral sense if accepted literally as true, inasmuch as they are libellous to the Deity. I propose, therefore, Secondly, that teachers be required, alike by School-boards and by parents, whenever such portions of Scripture are read,—(and they ought to be read, if only to show the advance we have made)—to make their pupils clearly understand that they represent only the imperfect notions of a barbarous age and people. That just as the Greeks had their supreme ruling divinity in Zeus, their divinity of song in Apollo, of war in Ares, of gain in Hermes, of storms in Æolus, of wisdom in Pallas, and of love in Aphrodite ; so the Jews, instead of distributing these functions among a number of distinct divinities, ascribed them all in turn, no matter how incongruously, as occasion required, to their own Jehovah. By turn he is a " man of war," he is " love," he is " fire," he " rides on the wings of the wind," and so on.

We cannot even accord to the Jews the credit, often claimed for them, of being, in a world of polytheists, the only pure monotheists. It is true that their institutions forbade the *worship* of more than one God; but they recognised the existence of many gods. They were monotheists in worship, but not in faith. Their Jehovah was a far too unsociable, exclusive, "jealous" God, to share their homage with others. He thus was made strictly in the image of the Jews themselves, the most exclusive of human races. That Baal and Chemosh, Ashtoreth and Molech, were all realities for them, is shown in frequent utterances ascribed even to Jehovah himself. And Solomon, though "the wisest of men," established their worship in Jerusalem. The Bible shows, too, by numerous instances, that the Jews were by no means satisfied with their own deity. The minds of their loftiest poets, indeed, occasionally, in their loftiest moods, rose to the conception of a deity, one and universal; but they did this in common only with the loftiest minds of all peoples, ages, and religions; those minds whose opinions have ever been regarded by the conventional and superstitious as atheistic and blasphemous, whether it be Socrates, Spinoza, Shelley, or Jesus.

But even if the Jews acknowledged but one God, they called him by various names; and it would be an additional safeguard against superstition if, in the new version, those names were preserved. In translating the Latin and Greek writers we never think of substituting God for Jupiter or Apollo. There is no valid reason for dealing differently with Jehovah, Elohim, Adonai, Shaddai.

This, then, is the whole conclusion :—

(1.) That the Bible should be admitted into the schools; but it must be a purified, an expurgated Bible; and (2.) That its reading must be accompanied by such "notes and comments" as will make it really conducive to the development of the Intelligence and Moral Sense of the scholars.

But to minister to these ends, it must be read with no adventitious solemnity that might specialise it as a superior authority, and invest it with a preter-educational character. For this would at once be to remove it from the category of legitimate educational uses, by exempting it from the operation of the normal digestive apparatus of the intellect. In short, to make the Bible useful for education, it must be taught *comparatively*. And as this implies the possession of a certain amount of *related* knowledge, it is clear that there is but very little of it that is suited to the very young or very ignorant.

XIV.

Now for the general principle on which these "notes and comments" should be based.

It is universally acknowledged that the human mind is endowed with a tendency to imagine the Deity as possessed in perfection of all the qualities which are recognised by itself as best. The strength of this tendency is ever in inverse proportion to the degree of the mind's development, being greatest in the most rudimentary stage of intelligence.

Investing the Deity with the attributes of personality, the finite mind cannot do otherwise than make God in its own image. The character of that image is the measure of our own moral and spiritual capacity. For, when by God we mean the ideal of our own imagination, it follows that the character of our God indicates the degree of our own development. Later on, when the mind attains a certain advanced stage of intellectual progress, we find our conception of Deity so transcendently enlarged, that no definition satisfies us, save one which recognises Him as the sum of all the *forces*, physical, moral, and spiritual, at work in the universe; the divine work, which we call Nature, being the sum of all *phenomena*. God the sum of causes, Nature the sum of effects. This is no dogma. It is only a definition of what we mean by God, what by nature.

For the purposes of early education, however, we have to deal with God in a moral aspect, as the Ideal of Humanity; the perfection towards which it is our highest function to strive. Wherefore, nothing can be more fatal to our moral progress than to have that ideal degraded to a low type of character. If we are to call him "Fool," who, denying cause and effect, says, "there is no God," (Ps. xiv. 1.) what are we to say of him who teaches that God is evil? What, again, are we to call those who, holding that God is absolutely good, and that a firm belief in that goodness is requisite to enable man to be good also, and who, moreover, desire to cultivate goodness in their children, yet hesitate not to put into the hands of those children narratives of impurity, cruelty, and deceit, and tell them that the perpetrators and their deeds were acceptable to, and indeed prompted by, the Deity? If the purpose of right education be to develop the moral sense, what sort of education is this? If another purpose be to develop the intellect, how is this end to be served, when the only way of escape that such teachers have, on being questioned by their perplexed pupils, lies in declaring it to be a "mystery," and so closing the doors of their intelligence the moment it begins to expand?

Keeping in mind the remarks I have made respecting the inevitable anthropomorphism of all imperfectly developed minds, you will perceive that it involves no reproach to the Jews that, in those early stages of human progress, they partook of the universal tendency, and constructed their God in their own image; that they credited him with the qualities, moral and immoral, which they found in themselves; and, in their total ignorance of natural law and phenomena, were more ready to seek the divine hand in departures from the regular order of nature, than to recognise it in its establishment and maintenance. It is thus that all early literatures necessarily contain prodigies and fables illustrative of the imperfect notions of their period. And so far from these things being true because they are in the Bible, or a reproach to the Jews in being untrue, the miracle really would have been if there were no miracles, no anthropomorphism, in the Scriptures. In this sense, therefore, it may be said that the truth of the Bible is proved by the untruths of the Bible.

Even if we give the Jews credit as having done their best for the honour of their god in thus constructing him in their own image, we assuredly cannot lay claim to similar credit for ourselves. For we have fallen infinitely below our own best, in the character we have assigned to our God. Think for a moment how marvellous is the anomaly we present. For six days of the week we avail ourselves freely of the wondrous results of the most advanced science and culture, philosophy and thought, of this nineteenth century after Christ, in which the labours of all former centuries have culminated, and we do this for our own advantage and enjoyment; and on the seventh day, when the honour of our God is concerned, we are content to jump back to the nineteenth century before Christ, and borrow for him both character and lineaments from a semi-barbarous Syrian tribe, whose whole literature proves their absolute incapacity to comprehend the simplest of his works in nature. And in their image, fitful and vengeful, we make our God, refusing him the benefits of the light we have gained. A wondrous feat of moral and intellectual athletics is this our weekly jump backward and then forward again.

The resolution finally passed by the London Board provides that "the Bible shall be read, and there shall be given therefrom such instruction in the principles of religion and morality, as is suitable to the capacities of children, no attempt being made to attach the children to any particular denomination."

Thus, the Bible is to be read "with notes and comments." If, however, these notes and comments are not to be of the kind I have just described, the Resolution means absolutely nothing. If the teachers are not to explain that Abraham, Isaac, and Jacob, Samuel, David, and Solomon, were, in respect of the acts which have been enumerated, exceedingly bad men, and that the deity who is said in the Bible to have approved of them, was but the imaginary local divinity of the Hebrews as represented by their priests, the Resolution is nothing but an illusion and a blind. If the teacher is not to say that Abraham was wrong to follow his impulse to sacrifice his son; Jacob wrong to cheat his nearest and dearest relations; Samuel wrong to revoke his sovereign's pledge of clemency, and rebelliously to set up a rival to him; David wrong to sacrifice the sons of Saul, and to order the execution of the man he had sworn to spare; if he is not to say that Jesus and the apostles were mistaken in expecting the early end of the world and re-appearance of Christ; that the story of his birth is a piece of mere paganism, and that many of the injunctions in the New Testament are not fitting rules for civilised life—the Resolution is utterly devoid of meaning. I am not saying that it may not be perfectly sound theology to praise Abraham and Jacob for these things, and represent the deity as approving of them, but only that it is neither good religion nor good morality; and it is not theology, but religion and morality, which, both by the Education Act and the Resolution, the teacher is bound to inculcate. Even if it be true that morality is based upon religion, the religion containing such theology can certainly not claim to be in any way connected with morality. And to teach it will be to go directly in the face of the Resolution which provides "that instruction be given from the Bible in the principles," not of theology, but "of religion and morality." Wherefore, when a question arises in the schools, such as that of the propriety of Abraham's compliance, of Jael's treachery, or of Caiaphas's counsel to offer up Jesus in human sacrifice as an atonement for the people;— the teacher acting in accordance with our definition and the Board's Resolution, will have no choice but to reply, "The justification of these actions belongs to the domain of theology. Morality unequivocally condemns them. And my duty here is to teach you morality."

And this, I think, settles the question which has been

raised since the passing of the Resolution, namely, the question, *Who* is to give Biblical or religious instruction in the schools, whether the ordinary teachers who are responsible to the Board, or the clergy or other persons specially appointed for that purpose by the various religious bodies themselves? The resolution declares that the children are to be taught, not theology, but Religion and Morality. To admit, therefore, independent teachers of theology, would be, in so far as such theology is in conflict with religion and morality, to admit teachers of irreligion and immorality, and would thus neutralise the Resolution of the Board, and the whole object of education, which, as cannot be repeated too often at this time, consists in the development of the intellect and moral sense.

Probably nothing could be put before the young more pernicious than the teaching of the official theologian. It was but the other day that a clergyman of the English Establishment preached a sermon to the effect that Jacob was quite right to cheat his father and brother because he knew that he should make a better use of the property than they would. No, however sound the *theology* of such teaching may be, and this is no rare or extreme instance, it certainly is not the teaching by which either the intelligence or the moral sense of children is likely to be developed.

XV.

So far from the simple and natural explanation which I have given of the incongruities and contradictions contained in the Bible, having been diligently promulgated by those who have undertaken to be its interpreters, our spiritual teachers have, on the contrary, during some three hundred years done their best to erect the Bible into an infallible standard, not merely of theology, but of religion and morality. Outvying the apostle who, in the excess of his zeal, cut off one ear, they have done their best to stop up both ears against the voice of reason and conscience. They forget that Jesus restored the injured organ.

It is true that an excuse for the existence of the popular theory, and for the tenacity with which it has held its ground, is not far to seek. It was natural that we should feel a high degree of gratitude towards the book which materially aided us in emancipating ourselves from the yoke of mediæval Papalism, and asserting our own individuality among the community of the nations. It was natural that our enthusiasm for the agent of our deliverance should lead us to place it high, even too high, in our regards. And so it came that we replaced an infallible, but discomfited, Pope by an infallible book; not perceiving that, if indeed it was a credit to the Bible to have made us free, we do the reverse of honour to it by allowing it to tyrannise over us in turn.

Again, in addition to being a grateful, we are an eminently prudent, folk. We prefer to be on with a new love before we are quit of the old. Hating anything like an interregnum, we cry, "The king is dead. Long live the king," without the interval of a moment. And so we continue to cling to the old accustomed dwelling, letting it crumble into ruin around us, rather than endure a brief season of discomfort while waiting for the rearing of a new habitation on its site. "If we give up the Bible as an infallible guide," it is asked, "to what are we to look in its place?"

Having at present to deal with facts, and not with fancies, there is no need to enlarge on the popular dogma further than to say that, not being contained in the Bible itself, but being unknown alike to the Fathers of the primitive Church, to the Reformers of the sixteenth century, and to the articles and formularies of both the Romish Church and the English, it must have its basis in modern innovation rather than in ancient authority.

I ascribe, then, the popular theory respecting the Bible in some degree to the causes I have named, but mainly to that instinctive monarchical tendency which leads the uneducated to distrust their own intelligence and moral sense, and require some palpable ruler and guide. " In their ignorance of the experimental character of human nature, men will seek infallibility somewhere; in an oracle, a priest, a church, or a book." This tendency has been, as a rule, sedulously fostered by governments and teachers. Once deprived of their Fetich, and roused from indolent acquiescence in its supposed commands, they cry out that their gods have been stolen from them, and fancy that the universe will collapse, because they are now forced to fulfil their proper vocation, and use their own faculties.

It was in virtue of this characteristic that the Swiss theologians of the seventeenth century maintained the inspiration of the comparatively recent vowel-points of the Hebrew text: that the early Christians ascribed a supernatural origin to the Septuagint; and the Council of Trent gave an authority superior to that of the original texts to the Vulgate, which attained such a height of superstitious respect that, according to Erasmus, some monks, on seeing it printed in parallel columns between the Greek and the Hebrew, likened it to Christ crucified between the two thieves. (Colloquies.) And it was even seriously proposed by the theological faculty of Mayence, in the 15th century, to make a total "revision and correction of the Hebrew Bible, inasmuch as it differed from the authorised Latin translation!"

Perhaps the most singular fact in connection with the popular doctrine is, that to doubt its accuracy has come to be treated as a piece of heinous moral depravity, and this even by some who ought to know better. When the eminent author of the "Christian Year" was consulted respecting a difficulty in the way of receiving it, felt by Dr Arnold, then a student, Keble's advice was "work it down! Throw yourself wholly into your parish or your school, and work it down!"* This simply meant, "ignore it;" as if faith consisted in the suppression of doubt, and conscientious scruples were demons to be exorcised.

Later in life, when pressed on the same point by Sir John Coleridge, who urged the subject on him as one that he was competent to deal with, adding that it promised shortly to become the great religious question of the time, Mr Keble, after endeavouring to evade answering, replied shortly that "most of the men who had difficulties on this subject were too wicked to be reasoned with."† Such was the answer of one of the most venerated of modern Sacerdotalists to a near relative of the great Coleridge, who (in the book I have already quoted) had pronounced the popular doctrine to be "superstitious and unscriptural."

"Ignore a conscientous scruple, or you are too wicked to be reasoned with!" Respect a dogma because it is a dogma, no matter how the reason and the conscience, nay, the Almighty himself, be outraged thereby! Submit humbly to authority, no matter how immoral its require-

* Stanley's Life of Arnold. † Coleridge's Memoirs of Keble.

ments! Ignore your scruples, and instead of manfully "facing your doubts" and "beating your music out," let your doubt remain, an unresolved discord, to jar evermore within your soul! To such straits are they driven who remain in bondage to "the weak and beggarly elements" of the popular orthodoxy. Surely it is time for us to say positively that we will not commit the minds and consciences of our children to teachers who will bring them up to regard sincerity as a vice, and crush at once both intellect and moral sense by superstition, popular or ecclesiastical.

XVI.

But though our immediate teachers in nursery, school and pulpit, have laboured assiduously to inculcate this dogma, it may safely be affirmed that, in addition to the vast range of authorities already named who reject it, there is not at this day a single scholar, (I do not say "learned divine," but scholar of acknowledged critical ability,) lay or cleric, orthodox or heretic, in Christendom, who holds it for himself. One and all, they recognise the existence in the Bible of, at the very least, a largely pervading element of human imperfection. It is true that Dr Hook in his "Church Dictionary" defines "Inspiration" as being "the extraordinary or supernatural influence of the Spirit of God on the human mind, by which the prophets and sacred writers were qualified to receive and set forth divine communications without any mixture of error," and asserts upon his own sole authority that in this sense the term occurs in the passage, "all scripture (is) given by inspiration of God." (2 Tim. iii. 16.) It is true that in this he is followed by Dr

Wordsworth and other prominent churchmen. But no critical scholar ventures to affirm that "Inspiration" is identical with, or implies, "Infallibility." On the contrary, their profoundest investigations only serve to demonstrate the truth of the conclusion patent to common sense, that humanity is so constructed as to be incapable of infallibility in the absence of means of verification; and that the being prompted by a "holy spirit," or disposition, by no means guarantees a man against error, however wide his spiritual range, or deep his spiritual insight.

But farther, even if the original text could be regarded as infallible, there is the fact that we do not possess that original text, and that the documents which claim to be derived from it, have passed through the hands of many copyists, each more or less accurate, more or less honest. And were the text certainly perfect as it is certainly most defective, there are still the difficulties of translation, difficulties which are, as every scholar knows, often absolutely insurmountable. For the language of different nations varies with their ideas, and their ideas vary with their institutions, associations, and habits; so that different languages frequently have no terms whatever in which to express the ideas contained in other languages. Many tropical tribes, for instance, have no words to express such things as *ice* and *snow*, because those things are altogether unknown to them. A translation, therefore, of the Bible into their language is, so far as ice and snow are concerned, impossible. "In the islands of the South Seas there were no quadrupeds until the first navigators took some pigs there, when the name given by the natives to the pigs, became the generic term for all four-legged animals. The horse was the big pig that runs over the ground. The cow was the great milky pig. The sheep the curly pig. We may imagine the feelings with which the pious translators of the Bible for the islanders found themselves compelled to use a corresponding designation for the phrase "Lamb of God." The Zulus of South Africa had no idea of God or a future state, and prized above all things flesh in an advanced stage of decomposition. Wherefore the missionaries in translating the Bible for them, and rendering the supreme good in their language, were obliged to identify God and heaven with rotten meat.

The same lack of corresponding terms exists more or less between all languages, as is shown by the fact that words and phrases are often transported whole from one language into another. Moreover, words used to express actions, principles, or qualities, in one language, often become concreted into persons and things by the genius of another. And in all languages, or nearly all, the same word frequently has many different significations. (As in English the words *box*, *band*, &c., have each half-a-dozen meanings.) It sometimes happens, therefore, that a translator has to be guided by what he is led by the context or some other criterion to think the passage is likely to mean.

Thus, in the passage, "Whosoever will save his life shall lose it: and whosoever will lose his life for my sake shall find it. For what is a man profited if he shall gain the whole world, and lose his own soul? or what shall a man give in exchange for his soul?" (Matt. xvi. 25, 26.) —the word rendered *soul* is precisely the same, article and all, with the word rendered *life*.

Again, for the word *spirit*, which is used by us in nearly a score of different senses, personal and impersonal, the

Greek equivalent, *pneuma*, generally, if not always, signifies the air, breath, or life. In the well-known passage in John, (iii. 8.) " The wind bloweth where it listeth, and thou hearest the sound thereof, but canst not tell whence it cometh and whither it goeth ; so is every one that is born of the spirit,"—the word rendered *wind*, and the word *spirit*, are identical, article and all, with each other. Yet the translators have given to the same word, occurring in the same sentence, two entirely different meanings. And, as if to justify this, the modern printers of the Greek text sometimes give a capital initial to the word which is translated *spirit;* thus in a measure altering the text to suit the authorised version.

Such was the imperfection of the ancient Hebrew for the purposes of expression in writing, that it was not until long after the Bible had been written that the distinction between the tenses of past and future was properly developed. It was in their confusion between these tenses that our translators, in the magnificent ode of Isaiah beginning, " Comfort ye, comfort ye, my people," produced the absurd and impious phrase, " She hath received at the Lord's hand double for all her sins," instead of the joyous assurance, " She shall receive . . . double for all her sufferings." (xl. 2.) It is easy to imagine the difficulty attending prophetic expression in a language which had no distinct future tense !

A very little reflection on the *modus operandi* of what theologically is called " Inspiration," will at once exhibit to us the fallacy of the popular notion. It can only consist of an impulse or impression on the mind, so strong as to make the individual receiving it, ascribe it to a preternatural source. But, however irresistible for him, the authority and character of the impression must still be determined, not by its strength in relation to his mind, but by its own intrinsic nature. A bad impression cannot proceed from a healthy source; neither does a strong impression imply accuracy of doctrine. It is under an irresistible impulse that the maniac mother flings her child down a well. It is under an impression so strong as to be for him an inspiration or divine revelation that the celibate takes his unnatural vow, the devotee starves himself into bad health, the Russian fanatic mutilates his body, and the Revivalist goes into convulsions of madness. Thus, whatever is claimed to be a divine revelation, must be referred ultimately to the test of the Intellect and Moral Sense, as the sole canon of criticism. Even the common notion that infallibility may be attested by the power to work miracles, must be disclaimed in presence of the instances ascribed in Scripture to magical or diabolical agency.

" Wherefore, although a man may have an overwhelming sense that something claiming to be God has spoken to him, it is clear, that unless he has a prior, personal and infallible knowledge of God,—a knowledge prior, that is, to his 'inspiration,'—he knows not but that it may be a demon assuming the garb of light, perhaps even one of those 'lying spirits' who are represented in the Bible as infesting even heaven itself, or a fantastic creation of his own excited fancy. It behoves him, therefore, still to judge the communication in his calmer moments by its own intrinsic character, and to deliberate upon the actions to which it impels him." The wider the range we learn to assign to Nature and the human faculties, the less becomes our necessity for seeking a preternatural origin for our ideas and impulses, and the more honour we pay to the divine worker and his work.

The prevalent readiness to distrust our own ability to perceive the higher moral facts of the universe, and our consequent liability to refer all revelation to the consciousness of men who lived ages ago, is, no doubt, attributable partly to our possession of so many ancient books which claim our attention, and draw our minds away from the contemplation of the direct action of the universe upon our own individual consciousness; and partly to the repressing influence of those sacerdotal interests which naturally repose upon traditional authority rather than upon living insight and reason.

The habit is one to be firmly checked if we would avoid the practical Atheism of banishing God and Truth from the living present to the dead past. "The creed or belief of any age is, at best, but the index to the height of the divine presence of Truth *in that age*." To adopt its limitations as our own, is to turn a deaf ear to the voice of that "Spirit of Truth" or Truthfulness, of whom it was said by one who himself drew all his inspiration from within, that "when he is come he will guide you into all truth." (John xvi. 13.) It is but a limited sway that this Spirit of Truthfulness has as yet obtained. Wherefore the effect of all dogmas,—whether formulated in creeds, catechisms, or articles of faith,—and their maintenance by oaths and emoluments, independently of intrinsic probability or any possibility of verification, is to arrest the natural development of Humanity and to disturb and retard the whole process of the evolution of the species, in regard to its highest functions. It is to give the world a base money-bribe to retain in its maturity the form, the garb, the dimensions, the *immaturity* of its childhood. Hear a recent utterance of one who, with whatever drawbacks, seeks still to combine the prophet and the poet, and thus, with "Songs before Sunrise," heralds the dawn of better times:

> A creed is a rod,
> And weapon of night:
> But this thing is God,
> To be man with thy might,
> To grow straight in the strength of thy spirit,
> And live out thy life as the light.*

The very word *Inspiration*, in its primary meaning, relates to the atmosphere. It is an ancient supposition that ideas are inhaled with the breath. A man found himself possessed of an idea or thought which the moment before he had not. Whence could it have come, if not in-breathed, or *inspired*, with the air? It was Pythagoras who conceived the idea that the vital process of the world is a process of breathing, the infinite breath or atmosphere of the Universe being the source of all life. An imaginative Oriental people readily, in their expressions, personified such supposed source of life and thought. We matter-of-fact Westerns go on to make such personification absolute and dogmatic. *Pneuma*, the air, becomes a personal spirit, or assemblage of spirits, and divinely "inspires" us: as in the old days of philosophy in Persia, under the influence of which, during, or after the Babylonish captivity, many of the Jewish sacred books evidently were composed,—the breath, or *Dir*, formed a linguistic basis for a personal Devil.†

Ideas in the air! Those who know what it is to

---

* Swinburne, very slightly altered.
† Cons. Donaldson's "Christian Orthodoxy:" Art. "Intermediate Intelligences."

crouch in the unhealthy confinement of close study, ever, as the Poet says,

> "With blinded eyesight poring over miserable books,"

till heart and head become heavy and dull; and then to betake themselves to seaside or mountain, where the fresh winds of heaven blow freely upon them, inflating their lungs, aerating their blood, and "sweeping the cobwebs from their brains," until the renovated organism becomes re-charged with creative energy, and ideas begin anew to spring up in the mind, revealing to it

> "Tongues in trees, books in the running brooks,
> Sermons in stones, and good in everything,"

—such as these can well appreciate the charming old fancy that peopled the air with ideas, and regarded every new thought as a separate spirit. It is only under theologic manipulation that such gentle poetry becomes steam-hammered into hard dogma, that existence is robbed of its charm, and millions of mankind are doomed to pass through life, and to leave it, without ever having been allowed to know how good the world really is.

But above and beside the questions of Inspiration, of Language, of Transcription, and Translation, there is the question of Interpretation. And, supposing all other difficulties surmounted, we are here met by an impassible barrier. For the proposition is nothing less than axiomatic, that "an infallible revelation requires an infallible interpreter: and that both are useless without an infallible understanding wherewith to comprehend the interpretation."

By such demonstration of the utter impossibility of infallibility, (in the theologic sense,) the ground is entirely cut away from beneath, not only all past, but all future superstitions. For, by annihilating "authority," it compels us to refer everything whatsoever to the criterion of the intellect and moral sense of man. There is now, therefore, no longer any space for "dogma."

XVII.

To the list of authorities already given, I propose to add a few representative names from the various schools of theologic thought within the Established Church.

The first is that of the Rev. Dr Irons, who, in his remarkable little volume, "The Bible and its Interpreters," declares that " any reasonable being who would accept the Scriptures at all, *must* take them on some other ground than that which identifies the written Word with God's Revelation. A more hopeless, carnal, and, eventually sceptical position, it is impossible to conceive." (p. 39.) Dr Irons, in this, follows the learned Bishop of St David's. Dr Thirlwall, whose recent noble protest against the dishonesty of sacerdotal bigotry in high places, in relation to the work of Biblical revision, may well raise our respect for him to veneration, as one who, in spite of his position, has dared practically to point the distinction between Morality and the prevalent Theology. In one of his Episcopal charges, Dr Thirlwall points out the fact that " Among the numerous passages of the New Testament in which the phrase *The Word of God*," occurs, there is not one in which it signifies the Bible, or in which that word could be substituted for it without manifest absurdity.

It is notorious that the popular imagination is wont to regard the same phrase, when used in the Psalms, as referring, if not to the whole of the Old and New Testaments, at least to the books ascribed to Moses and Samuel.

The late Dean of Canterbury, Dr. Alford, in his "New Testament for English readers," (p. 3.) says, "Each man reported and each man selected according to his own personal characteristics of thought and feeling."

Yet one other name, that of Bishop Colenso, whose critical analysis of the Hebrew text is allowed by scholars to constitute one of the most remarkable monuments of patient labour and sober judgment to be found in literature. These scholars, approaching the subject from opposite directions, agree in their main conclusions. Their immediate motives, however, differ considerably. The object of Dr. Irons is to force us back, in the search for Infallibility, to rely altogether upon "the Church." "Hear the Church," is his maxim. (Matt. xviii. 17.) But which Church? we must ask, and ask in vain. What saith the Church of England in her articles? "As the Churches of Jerusalem, Antioch, and Alexandria, have erred, so also hath the Church of Rome erred." (Art. xix.) Moreover, "General Councils. . . . . sometimes have erred." (xxi.) (It was a general Council that determined what books should form the canon of Scripture, and what should be rejected.) Can we wonder if the other Churches rejoin, as at least one of them has done, with anathemas, "So also hath the Church of England erred?"

The object of Dean Alford was to mediate between the two extremes of popular orthodoxy and the results of critical knowledge.

That of Bishop Colenso is simply to find out and state what is the fact, believing that such purpose alone is consistent with the deference due to the intellect and moral sense of man, to truth, and to God Himself. In one of his "Natal Sermons," he sums up the results of his labours by describing the Bible as containing the "Early attempts at History," the writers of which record, with the simplicity of childhood, the first imaginings of thoughtful men about the Earth's formation and history, and mingle with traditionary lore and actual fact, the legends and mythical stories of a hoar antiquity, yet tell us how men were "moved by the Holy Ghost," in those days, how they were "feeling after God," and finding Him, how the light shone clearer and clearer upon their minds, as the day-star of Eternal truth rose higher and higher upon them. . . . A human book, in short, though a book full of divine life. . . . . written, as Paul says, for our learning, but not all infallibly true." (i. p. 62, &c.)

But Dr. Irons and Bishop Colenso, while differing apparently so widely in their motives, yet have in reality the same object. The Bishop would force us back *directly* upon the Intellect and the Moral Sense. And Dr Irons would force us back upon them through the intermedium of "the Church," whatever that may be. For we need not entertain the uncharitable supposition, that he would have us substitute the authority of the Church for that of the Mind and the Conscience.

XVIII.

There is yet another authority to which it is necessary to refer, inasmuch as it is the highest present expression of the intellect and moral sense of the country applied to the regulation of human life in its secular relations.

We have seen that, so far as following Christ and his precepts are concerned, there are many respects in which both the Church and the world are palpably anti-Christian. The world rejects communism, celibacy, and contempt of knowledge; and both Church and world set at nought the most positive injunctions of Christ and of the Bible, as in taking medicine and in praying in Church. The practice of our Courts of Law is equally in opposition to the popular doctrine of an infallible Bible. Yet, with curious confusion, the popular mind still endeavours to concur with both; and judges still have the audacity to assert that the law of the land is founded on the Bible.

I will give an example or two.

You will remember the passages I quoted (p. 44.) in reprobation of the medical profession, and of those who, in illness, "Seek not to the Lord, but to the physicians." Well, we have among us a small sect calling itself after a Bible-phrase, "The Peculiar People." These hold that prayer is the only allowable resource for Christians in time of sickness. They do not refuse to cure themselves of hunger by food, of fatigue by rest, or to pick themselves up when they fall. They have no consistent theory or uniform practice respecting the relation of means to ends. But because a verse in one of the Epistles enjoins the calling in of the elders to pray over the sick, and declares that "the prayer of faith shall save the sick, and the Lord shall raise him up;" (Jam. v. 14.) they prefer to die sooner than call in a doctor, or take any medicine. Had the Apocrypha been thought fit by our Church to be included in the Canon, this sect would have had no existence, for the Book of Ecclesiasticus contains several warm commendations of medicine and medical men: saying, "Honour the physician. . . . for the Lord hath created him. . . . . the Lord hath created medicines out of the earth ; and he that is wise will not abhor them." (xxxviii. i. 1-15, &c.)

A short time ago, however, the neighbours of the people who are so very "peculiar" as to show their faith in the New Testament by their works, and to risk their lives on the strength of a vote in an ecclesiastical council, (that rejecting the Apocrypha,) were scandalised by observing that they had allowed a child to die without taking any human means to save it. An appearance in the police-court followed, when the leaders of the sect attempted to justify their conduct by an appeal to the Scriptures. But so diametrically opposed is the Spirit of our Law to that of the Sacred Books upon which our Law-Established Church is founded, that the magistrate, though he made allowance for the offenders on the ground of gross ignorance, flatly refused to receive their plea, and warned them that on a repetition of the offence, nothing would save them from being committed for trial on a charge of manslaughter. And his conduct received the approbation of a country calling itself Christian!

The other instance is that of the late case of "Lyon *versus* Home." This was an action for restitution of money obtained under false pretences ; and of course in an action of this nature the one thing to be proved is that the pretences under which the money was obtained, were false.

The defendant Home is one of a sect of persons who claim to hold intercourse with the spirits of the dead. The prosecutor Lyon is, (or was,) a believer in the doctrines of that sect, and in the defendant Home as one of its chief apostles. She is, (or was,) also a wealthy widow: and under the supposed injunctions of her departed husband, as made known to her through the mediumship of Home, she made over to Home a large portion of her property, I believe some £60,000, but the amount, however material elsewhere, is not material to our argument.

You will bear in mind that what I am about to relate occurred in a country whose laws maintain, at an enormous expense to its people, a Church called Christian, whose Sacred Books,—which are accepted by the whole nation officially as divinely inspired, and by the bulk of the nation individually as infallibly true,—repeatedly and unmistakeably affirm the leading doctrines of the sect to which the parties in this case belonged; namely, that intercourse is possible and frequent between the living and the spiritual world.

To quote some of the numerous passages involving this belief, there is the well-known story of the witch of Endor, in which the spirit of Samuel is represented as appearing to the witch, and delivering a discourse for the benefit of king Saul. (1. Sam. xxxvii.) There is the statement that at the crucifixion of Jesus, many of "the Saints which slept arose. . . . and appeared unto many." (Matt. xxvii. 52-53.) There is the story of the "Transfiguration," in which Moses and Elias, dead for hundreds of years, appeared to the disciples; (xvii. &c.) the conversion of Paul, in which Jesus himself, sometime dead, addressed Paul in an audible voice from heaven, (in the words of a Greek Play;*) (Acts ix. 4-6.) and the summoning back of the spirit of Lazarus to his body. (John xi. 25-43, &c.) There is the parable of the rich man in torment conversing with the spirit of Abraham in bliss, begging, with curious confusion between spirit and matter, that the spirit of Lazarus might be permitted

* The Bacchæ of Euripides.

to " dip the tip of his finger in water" and cool the rich man's tongue : or, in case the alleviation of suffering were not among the functions of the blessed, that the spirit of Lazarus might be sent back to earth to convert the five living brethren of the rich man; which last request was refused, not as the first was on the ground of its impossibility, but as superfluous and useless. (Luke xvi. 22, &c.). We read, too, of guardian angels, (Matt. iv. 4.) and "ministering spirits;" (Heb. i. 14.) and of a whole apparatus of intermediate intelligences existing between God and man. In the Acts we find certain pious Pharisees exclaiming of Paul, "if an angel or spirit hath spoken to him, let us not fight against God." (xxiii. 9.) John tells us to "believe not every spirit, but try the spirits whether they be of God." (1 John iv. 1.) Job, in thrilling language, describes a spirit as passing before his face and pausing to speak to him. (iv. 15, &c.) The practice of necromancy is forbidden in Deuteronomy, (xviii. 2.) its reality not being called in question; (though how the Jews reconciled it with their denial of the afterlife, does not appear.) The Gospels repeatedly refer to cases of possession by spirits, without specifying their nature or origin; and in Smith's Dictionary of the Bible, the fact of apparitions of the dead is regarded as being, for the Bible, past a doubt.

Such, on this point, are the tenets of the book which it is an article of faith with the very people whose law was invoked in the case of " Lyon *versus* Home," implicitly to believe. And yet, so far from any proof being required of the falsity of the defendant's pretences, they were at once assumed to be an utter and monstrous imposition; and the defence was laughed out of court, in face of the contents of the very book upon which the witnesses in it had been sworn: the book upon which our Religion is " by law established ;" and for the sake of inculcating which as infallible, we insist upon vitiating or crippling our whole system of National Education!

To these illustrations of the growing divorce between ancient credulity and modern Belief must be added that of Witchcraft; concerning the belief in which John Wesley said that "The Bible and Witchcraft must stand or fall together." While the anger excited among us by the devout utterances of the Prussian king over his late successes, may be ascribed in some degree to the fact that we are learning to repudiate the old notions which, recognising success as the test of merit, make Divine Providence the arbiter in human quarrels ; and in some degree to the consciousness of having ourselves been such eminent practisers in the same pietistic line as to make king William's conduct look very much as if meant for a caricature of our own.

Having paid some attention to the recent sittings of the Church Assemblies in Edinburgh, I have been pleased to observe symptoms of a growing respect for the authority of the Intellect and the Conscience in regard to matters of Faith, north of the Tweed. I have read that one clergyman declared his belief that the sacrifice of Christ was an atonement of sufficient value to counterbalance the misdeeds of Satan himself, and justify the Almighty in pardoning the Arch-fiend; and that another "elder" valued the character of the Deity so highly "that his hair stood on end at the notion that God could ever be reconciled to the devil." I take it as a hopeful sign that these two theologians should thus renounce all claim to judge such questions by the old dogmatic standards, and appeal instead to their own moral sense. They have only to carry the process somewhat further to perceive that the God who could create such a being as the devil *at all*, or who could require to be propitiated towards his own offspring by such a sacrifice as that of Christ *at all*, is no God worthy of being acknowledged or revered by any being possessed of a spark of intelligence or independence of spirit.

Lord Chesterfield once wrote to a friend, "Both Shaftesbury and I have been dead for several years; but we don't wish the fact to be generally known." In the same way very much of the Bible has been dead for some time. It still exists, but is outliving its influence for evil; and there are many who fancy themselves interested in keeping the fact from being generally known.

Yet that it is no chimera which I am encountering, has just been powerfully illustrated by a discussion in the House of Lords* in relation to University Tests; wherein it was declared, both by Lord Houghton and by the Marquis of Salisbury, that "the immense majority of the people of this country adhere to the authority and teaching of the Bible; their reverence for it being so absolute that any person who avows hostility to its doctrines is disabled, not only from holding any office connected with moral and religious teaching, but almost from any political office. And that no one can appear at the hustings with any chance of success, and announce that he does not accept the Bible."

XIX.

Sir John Coleridge was right when he said that this Bible question promised shortly to become the great

* (Debate of May 11th 1871.)

religious question of the time. It is so; not for the reason he then anticipated, but because the Bible, or rather the popular theory about the Bible, stops the way to our advance in all that favours the redemption, or constitutes the highest good, of a people.

By reason of this one impediment our whole system of national education "hangs fire;" while our systems of private education are neutralised or vitiated. It is therefore for those who are under no obligation to refrain from using their reasoning faculties; those who decline allegiance to any dispensation which imposes a penalty for putting forth a hand to sustain and forward that which they regard as the Ark of their country's redemption; (1 Chron. xiii. 9, &c.) those who believe that it is only through man working together freely and intelligently with man towards the highest moral ends, that real good is to be done;—it is for these, I say, to grapple with the difficulty, and if need be, to take the place of those who have hitherto been our teachers. If we are no longer to regard the Bible as a Fetich, to be adored, but not comprehended; if we are not to adopt as an article of Faith the suggestion of the flippant Frenchman, that the God of the Jewish Scriptures and of our own advanced intelligence and moral sense, is in reality one and the self-same Being;—that he was once as bad as the Jews made him out to be, but has improved with age and experience, (a suggestion I have lately heard seriously propounded by a clergyman in despair at the difficulties he found in the Bible)—then the solution which has now been proposed must be accepted by us: otherwise the intellect and the conscience must be rejected altogether as illusory and inventions of the devil; and some other criterion, and one which discards both intellect and conscience, must be sought for to regulate our judgment.

For my part, I think better of my countrymen than to believe that when once the truth is put plainly before them, they will long halt between the two opinions. I believe that when once the alternative is shown to them to lie between gross superstition and a rational religiousness,—they will no longer endure that their faith be only definable as *believing what they know to be untrue;* but will insist on their children being trained to subject all things to the test of a cultivated intelligence and moral sense. Thus trained, they will peruse the Bible, no longer as slaves, but in a spirit of intelligent appreciation, sifting out the germs of truth for themselves, and not scoffing at or rejecting the whole on account of the husks.

From henceforth the teacher in the schools of the nation must never forget that it is the purpose of his schoolroom to be the training-ground, not of any party or sect, but whereon to develop the faculties which later in life are to determine the nature of individual belief. To impart a bias, or to anticipate or prevent the formation of genuine, honest opinion, by the early instilment of dogma, is at once to stultify every principle of sound education, inasmuch as it is to repress the intellect and contravene the moral sense. Whatever the views which may be adopted in mature age by those who have been educated under the system I am advocating, there will be no cause to fear that they will be the worse for being founded in an intelligence and moral sense which have been thus rigidly trained in youth.

Shall it be said of our solution as was said by one upon first beholding the sea, " Is this the mighty ocean, is this all?" "Yes," we may confidently reply, in respect to our reliance upon the intellect and the conscience developed by rational education, "these are all." At first, indeed, you see from the margin but a small part of them. But only trust yourself to them: launch boldly out upon them: sail where you will with them, and they will bear you safely through the whole universe of being."

At present, for us in England, the issue lies with our School-boards. If their members are themselves ignorant of the simple law of human development in religious ideas, or are unworthily complacent to the ignorance and superstition of their constituents, generations may pass before the standard of education and religion is brought up to the standard of modern thought and knowledge. Generations may pass and the Bible will still be found the subject of hopeless contention, and source of fatal disunion and weakness. And generations long hereafter will find the country sunk deeper and deeper in ignorance and barbarism; while the nations which have sprung from our race, and speak our language, will have passed so far ahead of us that they can only look back upon "poor England" with pity and contempt as an effete and imbecile land, "whose prophets prophesied falsely, whose priests bore rule by their means, and whose people loved to have it so."

In Two Volumes, uniform, price 7s. 6d. each.

THE PILGRIM AND THE SHRINE,

AND

HIGHER LAW.

TINSLEYS, PUBLISHERS.

"In *the Pilgrim and the Shrine* is represented a youth escaping from the trammels of traditional belief, and laying himself wholly open to the influences of the living Universe, so as to allow his entire system of religious faith to evolve itself freely from the contact of external nature with his own soul.

"In *Higher Law* a similar method is applied to Morals."— PREFACE TO *Higher Law*.

NOW READY, THE THIRD EDITION OF

THE PILGRIM AND THE SHRINE.

IN ONE VOLUME. Price 7s. 6d.

OPINIONS OF THE PRESS.

"It is seldom the critic has the pleasure of reviewing a work so original, thoughtful, and entertaining. Whether we regard it as a book of travels, or the true history of a romantic life, or a thoughtful and philosophical essay, it is equally remarkable and attractive: and not the least charm of the work is the elegant and scholar like style in which it is written. The reader is compelled to sympathize with and love the man, however much the opinions expressed in the work may hurt the feelings. There is no disguising the fact that 'Herbert Ainslie's' ideas on Christianity, or some very similar, are held by a vast number of the most able men of the day, and certainly by a number of the best degree-men both at Oxford and Cambridge."—*Athenæum*.

"With an author who recognizes in the novelist the artist of our day, the praise or blame of sects is of little moment. 'All I have to do,' he says, 'is to create the truest, highest, and most needed work I can imagine, and leave it to find its own audience and speak its own message, without troubling myself about possible results. Such is the course dictated by the highest faith.'—We have dwelt so long on the story, simple as it is, that we cannot treat with anything like justice the really important part of the book—the mental pilgrimage that runs parallel with Herbert's actual wanderings. All throughout is this dualism, this subtle connexion between the physical and mental parts of his nature. It is as if he had declared for the extreme physiological school of philosophy.—There is a current of subdued Pantheism which sometimes breaks all bounds. He glories in the Californian pine-woods, and their message is in harmony with his faith. 'We follow the impulse of our nature. The deeper we strike our roots into earth, the higher we rise towards heaven.'—We need not say more to show that in the case before us we are abundantly satisfied, and that we recognize in the author of 'The Pilgrim and the Shrine' an artist who approaches very near to the ideal that his brilliant pages disclose."— *Saturday Review.*

"We welcome the graceful and temperate expression of the new tendencies which we find in these 'passages.' The merit consists in the sincere statement and attempted solution of the cardinal problem, how to reconcile the claims of individual conviction with the claims of social duty; how, in the surrender of the old traditional belief, to retain a devout faith, to regard the world as the true sphere of action, yet to live above the world in its worldlier aspects: to be at once the practical man that works and enjoys; the contemplative man that knows the order and the uses of the world; and the religious man in whom knowledge and work have not extinguished the sentiment of a holy ideal. 'Herbert Ainslie' argues calmly, analyses with a logical composure, and is playful, witty, and humorous when occasion permits. He is rich in experiences gathered from converse with outward life, or harvested by quiet meditation. In addition to the attraction that many will find in this tale of intellectual adventure, more entertaining matter will also be found, pictures of scenery, sketches of wild life, graphic descriptions. In its pages we meet with sagacious comment, bold conjecture, pleasant anecdote, or witty remark. The repose of the book is that of the 'noble grandeur' of the trees which our traveller invokes. The style is transparently clear, the language pure, natural, and of Greek-like beauty. The author has tried to realise his ideal of the novelist's mission. We hope to meet him again, and to see him approximate still more closely to his high standard, in the delineation of more complex scenes of life, and wider diversities of thought, feeling, and action."—*Westminster Review.*

"This is a powerful and original book, and no one can rise from its perusal without having obtained valuable food for reflection. It indicates with merciless accuracy those 'spots in our feasts of charity' which too often render such feasts formal, meaningless, and lifeless. . . . . It is not given to every youth who hesitates, from scruples of conscience, to enter the ministry of the Church, to taste the delightful perils of semi-savage life, and then to find consolation and repose in the arms of such a lovely and sympathetic woman as Mary Travers is depicted."—*Times.*

"'The Pilgrim and the Shrine,' one of the wisest and most charming of books, has reached a second edition. It contains some additions, a few admirable pages on bringing up children. It is very interesting to observe that most of the wisdom of the book comes from its simple candour. Following this like a religion, and constantly keeping his eye fixed on the exhaustless significance of the facts of our daily life, the author has produced a thoroughly good and edifying book. The native freshness and bright clearness of his style strike everybody."—*Westminster Review.*

"Sincere autobiography has always a profound interest of its own, and this book has that interest to its fullest extent,—and everywhere perfect purity and naturalness of feeling."—*Spectator.*

"The hero's adventures are all told with a great deal of artistic skill. We could easily select passages of rare brilliancy and beauty,—painted with a master's hand. But these form only secondary and incidental features of a book, the main object of which is to describe the passage of a soul, out of what the writer regards as a land of Egyptian darkness and bondage, into one of liberty and light.—The book may do good if it lead the Churches more earnestly to consider the best way of dealing with Sceptical inquirers."—*Nonconformist.*

"This clever and interesting book is a forcible expression, not, indeed, of what any human being ought, in our opinion, to feel, but unquestionably of what a great many human beings are at this moment feeling. It faithfully represents the state of bitter and rebellious indignation into which many minds, naturally neither irrational nor irreligious, have been driven by the theology of the Letter."—*Fraser's Magazine.*

"The most intelligible theory of such a book is that it aspires to do for English materialism what 'Sartor Resartus' did for German transcendentalism; that is, present a fair picture of it as revealed to a young and susceptive mind. It is a very interesting book as a book."—*St James's Magazine.*

"Accepting the Editor's disclaimer (of its autobiographical character) as made in all good faith, we can only suppose that the papers of a singularly gifted and daring mind have been put into his hands; unless, indeed we give him credit for a power of imaginative realization which, in respect of its descriptions of travel, surpasses the marvellous pictures of Mr Kingsley in 'Westward Ho,' and, in respect of his hero's processes of thought on theological, moral, and social matters, far transcends any psychological romance that we are acquainted with. Whatever the genesis of the book, it is a production of singular power and beauty, full of fascination to all who have thought at all concerning the great problems of our moral and religious life, or pondered the manner in which Christianity professes to solve them. . . . . As an exhibition of the processes of rationalistic thought, the book, to those really competent to sit in judgment upon it, is very instructive. Regarded as a mere book of travels, it has great charms."—*British Quarterly Review.*

"It were the greatest folly in the world to ignore the influence of such a work as the one before us. Be it for good or evil, the publishing of this book must have tremendous results on the thought and belief of all educated men. Wonderfully attractive as a book of travel and adventure, it is still more attractive and engrossing, philosophically, as the history of a soul struggling through all the narrowness of mere theology, into free thought and high aspiration. While we cannot agree with this most clever author, we feel a true and earnest sympathy with him. His life is a 'resurrection' life, ever rising from the past to the present and the future. There is much to help a true man in this book, much to trouble, but much that will advance him. If the 'Pilgrim and the Shrine' falls into the hands of some, it will lead them to be sceptical, and possibly make them think it is grand to be so. If it falls into the hands of many, even where they cannot entirely follow it, they will see a wider, grander, nobler ideal, than they had hitherto placed before them. The book is talismanic, and as Carlyle says of such books, will *persuade* men. We trust the effect of such persuasion will be a larger and broader belief in the love of God, and more firm faith in the divinity of humanity."—*Gloucester Mercury.*

"A clever, earnest novel, which some of its admirers regard as a sort of nineteenth century *Pilgrim's Progress.*"—*Examiner.*

"It is a very remarkable *Pilgrim's Progress.*"—*Eclectic Review.*

"An honest, earnest, true-hearted book."—*Echoes from the Clubs.*

"It would do hundreds of thousands of people good to peruse it."—*Daily Telegraph.*

"The work of a brilliant, clever, and ready writer."—*Standard.*

"But hardly likely to penetrate to those whose cruel creeds and chilly, dismal lives, he, with a fine enthusiasm, desires to change."—*Fortnightly Review.*

"Its aspects are so varied, and the whole so fascinating, from whatever point of view it is seen, that we are forced to pronounce it a very masterpiece."—*Brooklyn* (U.S.) *Union.*

By the same Author,

HIGHER LAW: A ROMANCE.

A NEW EDITION,

IN ONE VOL. UNIFORM WITH "THE PILGRIM AND THE SHRINE." Price 7s. 6d.

"As to the literary characteristics of *Higher Law*, readers of *The Pilgrim and the Shrine* will not need to be informed that it is a work of more than mere cleverness. Something like genius inspires it. The originality of its conceptions, the penetration of its criticisms, the beauty and enthusiasm of its style, its careful study of character, and the ingenuity and independence of its speculations, will commend it to the admiration even of those who differ from its conclusions the most gravely."—*British Quarterly Review.*

"Those who have read *The Pilgrim and the Shrine* will need no words of praise from a reviewer to recommend to them a new novel by the same author. . . The method of *Higher Law* differs from that of the *Elective Affinities*. Goethe breaks out into a great deal of grossness. In *Higher Law* the absolute purity of the characters is the great charm of the story. There is a subtle vein of Pantheism—the physical Pantheism of Goethe rather than the spiritual Pantheism of Shelley—running through the whole story, and along with it are touches of a mysticism which reminds us at times of the fancies of Novalis. Considered as a work of art the unity which pervades the story is beyond all praise."—*Echo.*

"Whether we agree or dissent we can still give the author the same praise for this as we gave him for his former work; that is to say, we can credit him with originality, boldness, and a capacity for philosophical reflection of no mean order. . . Bravery of this particular kind is so very rare that when we do meet with it it should be handsomely acknowledged."—*Athenæum.*

"Unless the reader is thoroughly acquainted with the great questions of the day, unless he thoroughly, too, perceives the tendencies of modern thought, unless he is at home with the last Biblical criticisms, appreciates the lessons of Darwin and Huxley in science, and has laid to heart the doctrines of the more advanced school of physiologists, much in this very remarkable book will be perfectly unintelligible. Yet the book will find a large number of readers, who, as time goes on, are sure to increase. . . But the most superficial reader need not be frightened away from it. If he is capable of admiring wit and humour, he will find both in some of the minor sketches; if he has any love for description, he will find charming pictures of scenery in Mexico; if, too, he is capable of appreciating what true love means, he will find himself in a spiritual atmosphere such as we know of in only one novel of the present day. The whole of the love scenes are painted with an exquisite sense of poetry and delicacy of feeling. . . That same purity of style and earnestness of tone, that same depth of philosophic reflection which marked *The Pilgrim and the Shrine*, may all be found, rendered still more attractive by the beauty of the story, in the present work. There is no novel, in short, which can be compared to it for its width of view, its cultivation, its poetry, and its deep human interest . . except *Romola*."—*Westminster Review*.

By the same Author,

JEWISH LITERATURE AND MODERN EDUCATION

BEING TWO LECTURES

ON THE USE AND MISUSE OF THE BIBLE IN THE SCHOOLROOM.

Price 2s. 6d.   THOS. SCOTT, Ramsgate.

"Excellent in substance and spirit, they indicate the right Use of the Bible in Schools. The author solves what is called 'the religious difficulty' fairly and rationally."—*Westminster Review*.

www.ingramcontent.com/pod-product-compliance
Lightning Source LLC
Chambersburg PA
CBHW030905170426
43193CB00009BA/743